THE ESSENTIAL ALKALINE

DIET COOKBOOK

2 Books In 1: 4 Reasons Why You Must Start Alkaline Diet and How it Can Help Change Your Life for the Better Through Consistently Consuming Healthy Food.

BY

Tilda Wheeler

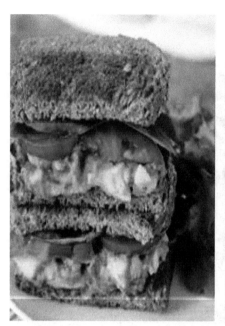

Copyrights Content Page

THE ESSENTIAL ALKALINE DIET COOKBOOK FOR BEGINNERS

THE ESSENTIAL ALKALINE COOKBOOK FOR BEGINNERS

THE ESSENTIAL ALKALINE DIET COOKBOOK FOR BEGINNERS

Table of Contents

INTRODUCTION

Alkaline diet carries many benefits. While you are on alkaline diet you have to balance acidity and alkalinity in your body.

Building up an alkaline diet doesn't imply that your diet will be without all corrosive framing food varieties. The main point of contention is balance. Both alkaline-shaping food sources and corrosive framing food sources are important for acceptable wellbeing. While we probably won't require some corrosive framing food varieties, as refined sugars or handled grains, we absolutely need satisfactory protein, and all proteins are corrosive shaping, regardless of whether from plant or creature sources. Too, certain nuts, (for example, Brazil nuts or walnuts) are corrosive shaping, yet they are nutritious food sources. Furthermore, while most vegetables alkalize, some are corrosive framing, like chard or peas—yet these food varieties are additionally nutritious.

1.　Best Vegan Pizza

Prep Time: 20 mins Cook Time: 15 mins Total Time: 35 mins Serves 3 to 4

Ingredients:

- 1 little head broccoli, florets chopped into little pieces, top of tail diced (½ cup)
- ⅓ cup split cherry tomatoes
- pieces from 1 ear new corn
- ¼ cup coarsely chopped red onion
- ½ jalapeño, daintily cut
- 4 oil-pressed sun-dried tomatoes, diced
- extra-virgin olive oil, for sprinkling and brushing
- 1 (16-ounce) chunk of pizza batter

- ½ cup new basil leaves
- 2 tablespoons new thyme leaves
- portions of red pepper drops
- ocean salt and newly ground dark pepper
- Cashew Cream

Guidelines:

1. Preheat the oven to 450°F.
2. In a medium bowl, join the broccoli, tomatoes, corn, onion, jalapeño, and sun-dried tomatoes and shower with olive oil and portions of salt and pepper. Throw to cover and taste. The vegetables ought to be all around prepared and very much covered with the olive oil so the vegetables are tasty all through the pizza.
3. Stretch the pizza batter onto a 14-inch pizza skillet. Brush the external edges of the mixture delicately with olive oil and spoon a couple of scoops of cashew cream onto the focal point of the batter, barely to extended it into a far layer. Appropriate the vegetables onto the batter.
4. Heat 15 minutes, or until the outside is golden, cooked through, and the broccoli is delicate and simmered. Eliminate from the oven and

sprinkle liberally with the cashew cream (if your cashew cream is too thick to even think about showering, mix in a little water). Top with the new basil, new thyme, and portions of red pepper pieces.

5. Veggie lover Pizza Variations
6. Spread conventional pizza sauce onto the mixture rather than the cashew cream.
7. Have a go at sprinkling this smooth veggie lover cheddar on top.
8. Utilize broiled tomatoes or cooked red peppers rather than the sun dried tomatoes.
9. Top your pizza with cured jalapeños for additional pop.
10.   Add spots of pesto rather than the new basil.

2. Romesco Cauliflower Sandwiches

Prep time 10 mins Cook time 30 mins Total time 40 mins serves: 4

Ingredients:

- 1 little head of cauliflower*
- 8 cuts of crusty bread or sourdough bread
- Modest bunch of salad greens
- A few bits of meagerly cut red onion
- 2 tomatoes, cut and prepared with ocean salt and pepper
- ¼ cup new parsley
- Extra-virgin olive oil
- Ocean salt and newly ground dark pepper

- Almond Milk Romesco Sauce (makes extra)
- 1 tomato, divided and cored
- 1 cooked red pepper, new or from a container
- ¼ cup toasted almonds
- 2 garlic cloves
- ¼ cup additional virgin olive oil
- 2 tablespoons Almond Breeze Almondmilk Original Unsweetened
- 1 tablespoon red wine vinegar
- ⅛ teaspoon red pepper pieces
- Ocean salt and newly ground dark pepper

Directions:

1. Preheat the oven to 450°F and fix a preparing sheet with material paper. Cut the cauliflower into ½-inch sections and spot onto the preparing sheet. Sprinkle with olive oil and portions of salt and pepper and heat for 30 to 35 minutes or until delicate in the center and golden around the edges.

2. Make the Romesco Sauce: In a blender, consolidate the tomato, simmered red pepper, almonds, garlic, olive oil, almond milk, red wine vinegar, red pepper chips, and a spot of

salt and pepper. Mix until smooth. Taste and change flavors.

3. Amass the sandwiches with the romesco sauce, salad greens, red onions, tomato cuts and simmered cauliflower and a couple of twigs of parsley.

Notes:

*depending on the size of your cauliflower, you may have more simmered cauliflower than you need to fill these sandwiches. Simply enjoy it as an afterthought or save it for the upcoming sandwich.

3. BBQ Jackfruit Sandwich

Prep Time: 15 mins Cook Time: 35 mins Total Time: 50 mins Serves 4 to 6

Ingredients:

- Bar-b-que Sauce
- 2 chipotle peppers + 2 tablespoons of sauce from a container of chipotles in adobo sauce
- ½ cup ketchup
- ¼ cup apple juice vinegar
- 2 garlic cloves
- 1 teaspoon Dijon mustard
- ½ teaspoon smoked paprika
- ½ teaspoon cumin
- Newly ground dark pepper
- Jackfruit
- 1 tablespoon extra-virgin olive oil
- 1 little yellow onion, meagerly cut
- ¼ teaspoon ocean salt
- 1 (20-ounce) can un-ready jackfruit, depleted
- ½ cup water

- Speedy Slaw
- 2 cups shredded cabbage
- 1/4 cup chopped cilantro
- ½ tablespoon lime juice
- ½ teaspoon olive oil
- Ocean salt and newly ground dark pepper
- For serving
- 8 slider buns or 6 burger buns
- Wanted trimmings: pickles, mustard, serrano peppers, and so on

Directions:

1. Make the BBQ sauce: In a food processor, mix the chipotle peppers, adobo sauce, ketchup, vinegar, garlic, mustard, paprika, cumin, and a couple of drudgeries of pepper until smooth. Put away.
2. Set up the jackfruit by pulling destroying the pieces with your hands (see photograph), disposing of any harder bits of the center. In a large skillet, heat 1 tablespoon of olive oil to medium heat. Add the cut onion and salt and cook, mixing once in a while, until delicate, 8 to 10 minutes, turning down the heat as vital. Then, add the shredded jackfruit and cook 5 minutes, mixing infrequently. In the event that essential, add a sprinkle of water to hold it back from adhering to the dish. Mix in the 1/2 cup water and half of the BBQ sauce. Turn the heat to low, cover, and let stew for 20 minutes. Eliminate the cover and mix in portion of the leftover BBQ sauce, holding the rest for serving.

3. Make the slaw: In a medium-large bowl, consolidate the cabbage, cilantro, lime juice, olive oil, and portions of salt and pepper.
4. Serve the sliders with the jackfruit, the excess BBQ sauce, the slaw, and wanted trimmings.
5. Bar-b-que Jackfruit Serving Suggestions
6. The bar-b-que jackfruit tastes extraordinary all alone, however to make it into a feast, I heap it onto custom made cheeseburger buns with a fresh cabbage slaw. It's really speedy to make – simply throw together meagerly shredded cabbage, cilantro, lime juice, olive oil, and a spot of salt. Top it onto the jackfruit pulled pork with bread and spread pickles, dill pickles, or cured red onions and whatever different trimmings you like!

4. Portobello Mushroom Tacos

Prep time: 15 mins Cook time: 15 mins Total time: 30 mins Serves: 2-3

Ingredients:

- Jalapeño Sauce
- ½, 1 or 2 jalapeños (contingent upon your zest inclination)
- 1 cup cashews, doused for in any event 3 hours, at that point depleted
- 1 cup water
- 1 tablespoon rice vinegar (or white wine vinegar)
- 1 tablespoon minced shallot
- ½ teaspoon garlic powder (or 1 clove of garlic)
- ½ cup chopped and stripped cucumber
- Crush of lemon
- Ocean salt and newly ground dark pepper
- ¼ cup chopped chives
- Tacos
- 2 portobello mushroom covers, stems eliminated
- Sprinkle of olive oil

- Sprinkle of soy sauce
- Sprinkle of balsamic vinegar
- 1 large avocado, cut
- 1 cup shredded red cabbage
- Modest bunch of cilantro
- 1 jalapeño, meagerly cut, optional
- 6 tortillas, flour or corn, warmed or barbecued

Guidelines:

1. Cook the jalapeños. You can do this over a gas oven, in a dry cast iron dish, or under your oven. Cook until the skin outwardly is dark and rankling. Eliminate from the heat, place in a bowl and cover with a kitchen towel or saran wrap for 10 minutes. When they're cool to the touch, strip off the skins (you can utilize your hands or a blade - it should fall off decently without any problem).

2. Eliminate the stem and seeds of your jalapeños and spot them in a blender with the cashews, water, vinegar, shallot, garlic, cucumber, lemon, salt and pepper. Mix until smooth and rich, adding more water if important to get your blender going. Taste and change flavors, adding more salt, pepper or lemon as you would prefer. Mix in the chopped chives. Chill until prepared to utilize.

3. Cut the portabello mushrooms. Spot them on a plate and shower them with olive oil, soy sauce, balsamic and newly ground dark pepper. Utilize your hands to cover the mushrooms on all sides.

4. Heat a barbecue or flame broil skillet to medium-high heat. Barbecue the mushroom

cuts on the two sides until burn marks structure, around 3-4 minutes for each side.
5. Collect tacos with mushrooms, avocado, cabbage, cilantro, cut jalapeños, if using. Present with jalapeño sauce.

Notes:
1. In case you're delicate to flavor, start by adding ½ of a jalapeño to your sauce ingredients. You can generally taste and add more. In the event that you've made your sauce excessively fiery, balance it by adding more vinegar. (In the event that it's too vinegar-ey, add a touch of olive oil).
2. Portobello Mushroom Tacos Variations
3. In the event that you don't have these accurate ingredients close by, go ahead and trade in what you do have! This taco filling is adaptable, and a wide range of varieties would function admirably. Here are a couple of my top picks:
4. Add something succulent. Top the tacos with diced cherry tomatoes or pico de gallo.
5. No cabbage? No concerns. Use romaine lettuce in its place.
6. Go for guac. Trade the avocado cuts for a major scoop of guacamole.
7. Add additional veggies. Fajita peppers would be phenomenal.
8. Make it heartier. Spoon in some cooked dark beans.
9. Increment the crunch. Sneak in diced red onion, salted red onion, cut radishes, or cured jalapeños!

5. Butternut Squash Stuffed Shells

Prep Time: 20 mins Cook Time: 35 mins Total Time: 55 mins Serves 4

Ingredients:

- 1½ cups cubed butternut squash
- extra-virgin olive oil, for showering
- 16 kind sized shells
- cashew cream
- 1½ cups crude cashews*, see note
- 1 cup new water
- 1 garlic clove
- 3½ tablespoons new lemon juice
- 1/2 teaspoon ocean salt
- newly ground pepper
- filling
- 4 cups new child spinach
- 1 cup disintegrated firm tofu
- 1 teaspoon dried oregano
- 1/2 teaspoon lemon zing
- touch of red pepper pieces
- 1 cup cashew cream, from the formula above

- ocean salt and newly ground pepper

Directions:
1. Preheat the oven to 350°F and fix a preparing sheet with material paper. Throw the butternut squash with a sprinkle of olive oil and a couple of liberal portions of salt and pepper. Cook until golden brown, 20 to 25 minutes.
2. Make the cashew cream: Blend together the depleted crude cashews, new water, garlic, lemon juice, 1/2 teaspoon salt and pepper.
3. Make the filling: In a medium skillet, heat a sprinkle of olive oil over medium heat. Add the spinach in increases, alongside a spot of salt, and sauté until all the spinach is consolidated and shriveled. Eliminate from heat and let cool somewhat. Press out any abundance fluid and slash. In a medium bowl, consolidate the spinach with the disintegrated tofu, oregano, lemon zing, red pepper chips, at any rate 1/4 teaspoon salt, newly ground dark pepper and 1 cup of cashew cream. Season to taste, adding more salt and pepper as wanted.
4. Heat a large pot of salted water to the point of boiling. Add the shells and cook as per the bundle directions until still somewhat firm. Channel.
5. Amass the shells. Spread ¼ cup of the held cashew cream on the lower part of a 11x7-inch heating dish. Fill each cooked shell with a portion of the filling and a couple of 3D shapes of butternut squash, and spot into the preparing dish. Shower a little olive oil over the shells, cover with foil, and prepare for 15

minutes, or until heated through. Eliminate from the oven and present with the excess cashew cream.

Notes:
1. *Depending on your blender, you might need to absorb the cashews water for a couple of hours (or overnight) with the end goal for them to get rich when pureed. Channel and wash when prepared to utilize. On the off chance that using a Vitamix blender or comparative, drenching isn't required.
2. Stuffed Shells Serving Suggestions
3. I like to serve my stuffed shells with touches of additional cashew cream to truly take them over the top. While this formula is tasty on any evening, it'd be particularly great as a veggie lover primary course at Thanksgiving or an occasion supper.

6. Cream of Mushroom Soup

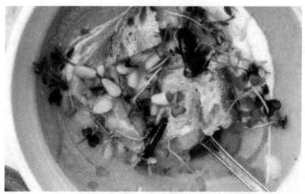

Prep Time: 10 mins Cook Time: 30 mins Total Time: 40 mins Serves 4 to 6

Ingredients:

- 2 tablespoons extra-virgin olive oil, in addition to additional for sprinkling
- 2 medium leeks, white and light green parts, cut (2 cups)
- 2 celery stems, diced
- 16 ounces cremini mushrooms, chopped
- 2 tablespoons tamari
- ¼ cup dry white wine
- 2 large garlic cloves, chopped
- 2 tablespoons new thyme leaves
- 4 cups vegetable stock
- 1 pound cauliflower, broken into florets (5 cups)
- 1 teaspoon Dijon mustard
- 1 tablespoon balsamic vinegar
- Ocean salt and newly ground dark pepper
- Beating/serving choices:
- Sprinkle of coconut milk

- Hard bread, toasted as bread garnishes or served as an afterthought
- Extra mushrooms, sautéed
- Toasted pine nuts
- Microgreens or delicate thyme leaves

Guidelines:
1. Heat the oil in a large pot over medium heat. Add the leeks, celery, ¼ teaspoon salt, and cook 5 minutes. Add the mushrooms and cook until delicate, 8 to 10 minutes more.
2. Mix in the tamari, wine, garlic, and thyme and cook for 30 seconds to 1 moment, or until the wine has vanished. Add the stock and the cauliflower.
3. Stew revealed for 20 minutes, or until the cauliflower is delicate. Move to a blender, add the mustard and vinegar, and mix until smooth. Season to taste and present with wanted toppings.
4. Cream of Mushroom Soup Serving Suggestions
5. On the off chance that you need to take this cream of mushroom soup over the top, don't avoid the embellishments! Crunchy fixings like custom made bread garnishes, broiled or sautéed mushrooms, and toasted pine nuts offer a tasty differentiation to its smooth, delicious surface. I additionally prefer to add a sprinkle of spices or microgreens for something new and a shower of coconut milk or olive oil for additional lavishness.
6. Serve your cream of mushrooms soup with natively constructed focaccia.

7.   Vegetarian Pho

Prep time: 10 mins Cook time: 40 mins Total time: 50 mins Serves: 2

Ingredients:

- 2 star anise
- 1 cinnamon stick
- 1 tablespoon entire peppercorns
- ¼ teaspoon entire cloves
- 5 cups water
- ½ little yellow onion, cut into 1" pieces
- 2 garlic cloves, squashed
- 1 2-inch piece of new ginger, cut down the middle
- 4 ounces shiitake mushrooms, stems eliminated and saved
- ¼ cup tamari, more to taste
- 1 tablespoon rice vinegar, more to taste
- 2 scallions, finely chopped
- 2 child bok choy, cut longwise into quarters
- ½ cup frozen edamame
- 4 ounces cooked rice noodles

For serving:
1. Lime cuts

2. Mung bean sprouts
3. New spices: basil, mint, as well as cilantro
4. Sriracha, cut thai chiles, or cut jalapeños

Directions:
1. In a medium pot over low heat, consolidate the star anise, cinnamon stick, peppercorns, and cloves and mix until fragrant, around 30 seconds.
2. Add the water, onion, garlic, ginger, and the stems of the shiitake mushrooms. Stew for 20 minutes, at that point strain and return the fluid back to the pot.
3. Cut the shiitake mushroom covers and add them to the pot alongside the tamari, rice vinegar, and scallions. Stew 15 minutes.
4. Add the bok choy and edamame and cook until delicate, 5-8 minutes. Taste and season with more tamari for profundity of flavor, and more rice vinegar for tang, as wanted.
5. Spoon the soup into 2 dishes over the cooked rice noodles. Present with the lime cuts, sprouts, spices, sriracha, bean stew peppers, and more tamari as an afterthought.
6. Veggie lover Pho Recipe Tips
7. Try not to avoid the embellishments. At the point when you request pho at a Vietnamese eatery, it will consistently accompany new spices, bean sprouts, lime, chiles, as well as sauces as an afterthought. In spite of the fact that they're introduced as trimmings, these trimmings are a fundamental piece of preparing the soup. Mix them into the hot stock for rich profundity of flavor. If you were

to ask me, this is the most awesome aspect of eating pho. You can prepare it exactly how you like it!

8. Modify it! I love this veggie lover pho formula as composed, yet go ahead and alter it as you would prefer. Add prepared or seared tofu for a heartier soup or supplant the bok choy with spinach or shredded Napa cabbage. On the off chance that you can't discover shiitake mushrooms, use cremini or clam mushrooms in their place. For a lighter alternative, preclude the noodles, or supplant them with zucchini noodles.

9. Make it ahead. This vegetarian pho formula serves two, yet in the event that you need to have extras, twofold it. I suggest putting away the stock independently from the noodles and vegetables. Something else, the noodles will ingest the stock in the ice chest. I additionally prefer to cook new bok choy regardless of whether I'm reheating the stock. That way, it holds its energetic green tone.

8.   Spiralized Daikon "RIce Noodle" Bowl

Cook time: 10 min Prep time: 20 min Serves: 2 major dishes, or 4 little

Ingredients:

- 8 ounces extra-firm tofu, cut into 3D squares
- 1 daikon, in any event 2" distance across and around 5" long
- 1 medium cucumber
- 2 carrots, stripped into strips
- 2 radishes, daintily cut
- ½ avocado, diced
- ¼ cup cilantro
- ¼ cup mint leaves
- 2 scallions, daintily cut
- 2 tablespoons toasted and chopped cashews
- extra-virgin olive oil
- ocean salt
- sriracha
- lime wedges, for serving
- Sauces: Tamari-lime and Creamy cashew

- 2 tablespoons tamari
- 2 little garlic cloves, minced
- 4 teaspoons new lime juice
- 4 teaspoons rice vinegar
- 1 tablespoon natural sweetener (or maple or agave)
- ¼ cup water
- 1½ tablespoons rich cashew spread (or peanut butter)

Guidelines:

1. Preheat the oven to 400°F. Line a preparing sheet with material paper and spread the tofu on the container. Throw with a shower of olive oil and liberal portions of salt. Prepare for 15 to 17 minutes or until golden brown around the edges. Eliminate from the oven and throw with a spurt of sriracha.
2. Make the sauces. In a little bowl, combine as one the tamari, garlic, lime juice, rice vinegar, sugar and water. Empty portion of the sauce into another little bowl. Whisk that half with the cashew margarine. Season to taste and save.
3. Utilize a spiralizer (or a julienne peeler) to cut the daikon and cucumber into "noodles." Portion the noodle vegetables into two dishes and top with the carrot strips, radish cuts, diced avocado, cilantro, mint, scallions, tofu, and cashews.
4. Serve the dishes with both the tamari-lime and velvety cashew sauce and lime wedges as an afterthought.

Notes:

In case you're not a fanatic of tofu, sub in another protein of decision.
On the off chance that you can't discover daikon, sub zucchini noodles

Tips:

Serve these dishes with a splendid, tart sauce. This one is made with lime, rice vinegar and tamari – it's pungent in that great fish-sauce-esque route yet without fish sauce. I likewise made a rich cashew sauce to serve as an afterthought. I know, two sauces seems as though additional work, however I just blended some of sauce #1 with cashew spread (you could likewise utilize peanut butter), and presto – 2 sauces. The main sauce is light, and the velvety cashew sauce is rich, so they cooperate pleasantly.

9. Sesame Noodle Bowl

Prep time: 20 min Cook time: 5 Serves: 2 to 3

Ingredients:

- Dressing/sauce
- 2 tablespoons white miso paste
- 2 tablespoons rice vinegar
- 2 tablespoons tamari
- ½ tablespoon toasted sesame oil
- (besides overabundance juice from the orange beneath)
- Bowls
- 1 medium orange
- 2 cups shredded red cabbage
- 3 ounces soba noodles, cooked, depleted, and rinsed* (see note)
- Extra-virgin olive oil, for showering
- ⅓ cup chopped scallions (around 3)
- 1 cup snap peas, de-stringed and chopped
- 8 ounces shiitake mushrooms, stemmed and cut
- 7 ounces prepared tofu, cut or cooked protein of decision

- Sesame seeds
- Small bunch of new spices, cilantro or mint, optional
- Ocean salt

Directions:
1. Make the dressing: In a little bowl, whisk together the miso, rice vinegar, tamari, and sesame oil until joined. Cut the sections from the orange, put away, and crush the overabundance juice from the orange into the sauce.
2. Make the dishes: Divide the red cabbage among a few dishes. Shower with a portion of the dressing and throw delicately to cover. Spot the cooked soba alongside the cabbage in the dishes.
3. In a skillet, heat a shower of olive oil and add the scallions and snap peas and cook, throwing until gently rankled yet energetic green, for around 2 minutes. Eliminate and add to the dishes.
4. Add more olive oil to the dish and add the mushrooms and a touch of salt and cook until the mushrooms are delicate, around 8 minutes. Split the mushrooms between the dishes and top with the orange portions, tofu, sesame seeds, and spices if using. Sprinkle with a tad bit of the leftover dressing and serve the lay as an afterthought. (Note: the dressing is somewhat on the pungent side so a tad goes far - add it to taste and save any extra for servings of mixed greens/bowls later in the week).

Notes:

1. *Cook your soba noodles as indicated by the bundle directions. Channel and flush them to eliminate overabundance starches. This aides them from bunching. In the event that they begin to stay together, throw them with a smidgen of sesame oil.

2. Noodle Bowl Variations

3. Bowl recipes are about the parts, so in many cases, they're unimaginably adaptable. This noodle bowl is no exemption. In the event that you don't have or don't care for one of the ingredients in this formula, go ahead and trade in something different. Here are a couple of ideas:

4. The veggies: I utilized red cabbage, sautéed mushrooms, and snap peas, yet cucumbers, snow peas, carrots, radishes, whitened asparagus, broiled broccoli, or simmered Brussels fledglings would be incredible decisions as well.

5. The natural product: I love the succulent orange fragments here, yet diced mango would be acceptable as well. You could likewise skip it, or add cured ginger for pop.

6. The protein: This formula calls for prepared tofu, however shelled edamame, fresh broiled chickpeas, or heated tempeh would be comparable.

7. The sauce: I make a simple mix together sauce with miso, sesame oil, squeezed orange, rice vinegar, and tamari or soy sauce, yet my 5-fixing nut sauce would work here as well.

8. A bonus: I top this bowl with new cilantro, mint, and green onions. Go ahead and utilize only one, or attempt new basil all things considered.

10. Vegan Corn Chowder

Prep time: 15 mins Cook time: 20 mins Total time:
35 mins Serves: 4-6

Ingredients:
- 1 tablespoon extra-virgin olive oil
- 1 medium yellow onion, chopped
- 3 garlic cloves, minced
- 2 ribs celery, chopped
- 1 Yukon gold potato, chopped
- 4 ears new sweet corn, husked
- 1 red pepper, diced
- ½ teaspoon celery salt
- ½ teaspoon smoked paprika
- 1 tablespoon sherry vinegar, or white wine vinegar
- 2 cups vegetable stock
- 1 (14-ounce) can light coconut milk (or 1¾ cups entire milk)
- Ocean salt and newly ground dark pepper
- Chopped chives, for decorate
- Hold some corn parts and diced red pepper for decorate (optional)

Guidelines:
1. Heat the olive oil in a large dutch oven over medium heat. Add the onion and a couple of portions of salt.
2. Cook until delicate, at that point add the garlic, celery, and potatoes.
3. Cut the pieces off the corn, at that point utilize the rear of your blade to scratch the juices off of the corn cob and add to the pot. Add the red pepper, celery salt, paprika, a touch of salt, dark pepper, and mix. Cook until the potatoes are somewhat softened, around 5 minutes, at that point add the sherry vinegar, vegetable stock, and coconut milk.
4. Cover and stew until the potatoes are delicate, around 15 additional minutes. Let cool marginally, at that point move a large portion of the soup to a blender. Mix until smooth at that point return it back to the pot and mix.
5. Taste and change flavors and present with chopped chives.

Tips:
1. Incredible veggie ingredients are the foundation of this soup, however these means are fundamental for making it smoky, fulfilling, and tasty:
2. After you cut the portions off cobs of new sweet corn, utilize the rear of your blade to scratch the juices off the cob. Add this dull, smooth fluid to the chowder to make it extra velvety and rich.
3. Mix a large portion of the soup, and leave the rest stout. In light of the starches in new corn and potatoes, these vegetables mix into a

delectable rich stock. I like to mix a piece of the chowder to make this smooth base and leave the rest thick for surface.

4. Remember to embellish. Save a couple of crude corn bits and bits of diced red pepper to sprinkle over bowls of chowder. They'll make the ideal fresh differentiation to the velvety soup. For extra smoky flavor, take a stab at garnish it with coconut bacon or tempeh bacon bits!

11. Roasted Red Pepper Soup

Prep Time: 10 mins Cook Time: 35 mins Total Time: 45 mins Serves: 4

Ingredients:

- 1/4 cup extra-virgin olive oil, separated, in addition to additional for sprinkling
- 1 medium yellow onion, chopped
- 2 garlic cloves, chopped
- 1 little fennel bulb, coarsely chopped
- 3 medium carrots, chopped
- 1 tablespoon new thyme leaves
- 2 tablespoons balsamic vinegar
- 3 jostled simmered red chime peppers
- 1/4 cup cooked cannellini beans, depleted and flushed
- 2 tablespoons tomato paste
- 4 cups vegetable stock
- 1/2 to 1 teaspoon ocean salt
- 1/2 teaspoon newly ground dark pepper
- 1/2 teaspoon red pepper drops, optional

For Serving (all optional):

1. 1 bumped simmered red pepper, diced

2. Finely chopped parsley
3. Portions of red pepper drops
4. Microgreens
5. Warm roll

Guidelines:
1. Heat 2 tablespoons olive oil in a large pot over medium heat. Add the onion and portions of salt and pepper and cook until clear, around 5 minutes.
2. Add the garlic, fennel, carrots, and thyme leaves. Mix and cook until the carrots start to relax, around 10 minutes.
3. Add the balsamic vinegar, red peppers, beans, tomato paste, stock, and 1/2 teaspoon salt. Stew until the carrots are delicate, 15 to 20 minutes.
4. Add the stewed soup to a fast blender with the leftover 2 tablespoons olive oil and puree until smooth. Season with more salt and pepper, to taste. On the off chance that you might want more punch, add a couple of more drops of balsamic, to taste. On the off chance that you might want a little heat, add 1/2 teaspoon red pepper pieces.
5. Present with liberal showers of olive oil, wanted enhancements, and warm loaf.

Serving Suggestions:
Like most soups, you can make this one ahead and save it in the refrigerator for a couple of days – the flavors simply improve and better. It likewise freezes well, so make it early and get it together for work day snacks

12. Easy Coconut Curry

Prep Time: 15 mins Cook Time: 35 mins Total Time: 50 mins Serves 4

Ingredients:

- 1 tablespoon coconut oil
- 1 cup chopped yellow onion
- 2 garlic cloves, minced
- ½ teaspoon ground new ginger
- ½ teaspoon cumin
- ¼ teaspoon coriander
- ¼ teaspoon turmeric
- ¼ teaspoon cardamom
- 1 teaspoon ocean salt
- 2 cups cubed butternut squash
- 3 red Thai chiles, or 1 serrano, or ½ jalapeño, meagerly cut
- 2 cups cauliflower florets
- 1 can full-fat coconut milk
- 1 tablespoon new lemon juice
- 1 tablespoon new lime juice, in addition to lime wedges for serving
- 4 cups new spinach

- ½ cup new or frozen peas
- Newly ground dark pepper

For serving:
- 2 cups cooked basmati rice
- a couple of large modest bunches of new basil or cilantro
- Naan bread, optional

Directions:
1. Heat the oil in a large Dutch oven over medium heat. Add the onion and cook until delicate and very much browned, around 10 minutes, diminishing the heat to low partially through.
2. In a little bowl, combine as one the garlic, ginger, cumin, coriander, turmeric, cardamom, and salt. Put away.
3. Add the butternut squash and chiles to the pot, mix, and cook for 5 minutes. Mix in the cauliflower and afterward add the coconut milk and the flavor blend. Cover and stew for 20 minutes or until the vegetables are delicate.
4. Add the lemon juice, lime juice, spinach, peas, and mix. Taste and change flavors, adding extra lime squeeze, salt, and pepper, as wanted.
5. Serve the curry over the rice with new basil, naan bread, whenever wanted, and lime wedges as an afterthought.
6. Vegetable Curry Recipe Variations
7. This butternut and cauliflower curry formula is entirely adaptable, so I urge you to utilize it as a layout. Here are a few plans to switch things up:
8. Utilize various veggies. On the off chance that you don't have butternut squash, utilize yams. Assuming you don't have cauliflower, use

broccoli. Green beans, carrots, chime peppers, and potatoes would be extraordinary here too.

9. In the event that you need more heat, zest it up. Add additional chiles or more turmeric, ginger, cardamom, cayenne, or red pepper chips.

10. Fluctuate how you serve it. You can serve this curry with basmati rice, brown rice, cauliflower rice, or even quinoa. You can likewise redo it with a protein that you like in your curry.

13. Tomatillo Salsa Verde

Prep Time: 5 mins Cook Time: 25 mins Total Time: 30 mins

Ingredients:

- 6 medium tomatillos
- 1/4 medium yellow onion, cut into large pieces
- 1 serrano or jalapeño pepper, stemmed* (see note)
- 2 garlic cloves, unpeeled, enveloped by foil
- 1/2 tablespoons extra-virgin olive oil
- 1/2 tablespoons new lime juice
- ¼ cup chopped cilantro
- 1/2 to 3/4 teaspoon ocean salt to taste

Directions:

1. Preheat the oven to 450°F and fix a heating sheet with material paper.
2. Eliminate the husks from the tomatillos and flush under cool water to eliminate the tenacity. Spot the tomatillos, onion and pepper on the preparing sheet, sprinkle with the olive

oil and a liberal touch of salt and throw. Spot the wrapped garlic on the container. Broil for 15 minutes or until the tomatillos are delicate.

3. Open up the garlic from the foil, strip it, and spot in the bowl of a food processor. Add the broiled vegetables, lime juice and cilantro and heartbeat. On the off chance that your salsa is excessively thick, add 1 to 2 tablespoons water to thin to wanted consistency. Season to taste.

4. Present with chips or with your number one Mexican formula.

Notes:
*If you're delicate to flavor, start by adding HALF of the pepper and add the rest to taste. On the off chance that you've made your salsa excessively fiery, have a go at adding a couple of sprinkles of white wine vinegar to restrain the heat.
Variety: make this salsa velvety by mixing in 1 little ready avocado.

Tips:
1. Get out the chips and begin scooping! Serve it with guacamole, pico de gallo, and margaritas.

2. Use it as a sauce for anything you're barbecuing or cooking

3. Make tacos! Salsa verde will energize any barbecued or simmered veggie taco filling. I additionally love mixing an avocado with my tomatillo salsa to make a smooth variety for tacos.

4. Make a burrito bowl by serving it over beans, rice (or cauliflower rice), and avocado

5. Save some for breakfast and scoop it onto eggs, present with a frittata, or scoop into a speedy breakfast taco.

14. Rosemary Focaccia

Prep Time: 20 mins Cook Time: 1hr 40 mins
Total Time: 2hrs Serves 8 to 10

Ingredients:

- 1¾ cups warm water, 105° to 115°F
- 1 (¼-ounce) bundle dynamic dry yeast, (2¼ teaspoons)
- 1 tablespoon unadulterated sweetener
- 3½ cups universally handy flour, in addition to additional for manipulating
- 1½ cups entire wheat flour
- 1 tablespoon ocean salt
- ½ cup extra-virgin olive oil, in addition to additional for brushing
- 1 bulb Roasted Garlic, optional
- 2 tablespoons chopped rosemary
- ½ teaspoon red pepper drops, optional

Guidelines:

1. In a medium bowl, mix together the water, yeast, and sugar. Put away for 5 minutes, until the yeast is frothy.

2. In the bowl of a stand blender fitted with a batter snare connection, place the flours, salt, ¼ cup of the olive oil, and the yeast combination and blend on medium speed until the mixture shapes a ball around the snare, 5 to 6 minutes.
3. Move the mixture to a softly floured surface and ply a few times, sprinkling with more flour, depending on the situation, and structure into a ball. Brush a large bowl with olive oil, and spot the mixture inside. Cover with cling wrap and put away to ascend until multiplied in size, 40 to 50 minutes.
4. Coat a 10 × 15-inch rimmed heating sheet with the leftover ¼ cup olive oil. Punch the batter down, move to a delicately floured surface, and massage a few times. Spot the mixture in the dish and press to spread it out to the container's edges. Flip the batter over and spread it to the edges once more. Make spaces with your fingers, each couple of inches separated, everywhere on the batter. Cover the heating sheet with cling wrap and permit the batter to ascend until it has multiplied in size, around 40 minutes.
5. Preheat the oven to 425°F. Eliminate the saran wrap. Slice the cooked garlic cloves down the middle and drive them into the outside of the batter. Sprinkle with the rosemary, and red pepper drops, and heat for 20 minutes, until golden brown.

Focaccia Recipe Tips:

1. Allow the batter to rise some place warm. Since yeast reacts to warmth, allowing your mixture to ascend in a warm spot will yield the best outcomes. We like to put our own on a bright windowsill!
2. Freeze additional items. This bread freezes truly well! Cut the prepared focaccia into squares and freeze them in an impenetrable compartment for up to a couple of months. I like to keep a reserve close by to fill in as a simple side with servings of mixed greens or soups.
3. Change the flavors! We love this basic broiled garlic and rosemary focaccia bread, yet different fixings would be scrumptious here also. Have a go at trading the rosemary for sage or thyme leaves, or use olives, sun dried or simmered tomatoes, or daintily cut Meyer lemon instead of or notwithstanding the broiled garlic.

15. Roasted Garlic Mashed Potatoes

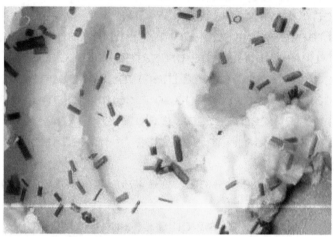

Prep Time: 10 mins Cook Time: 1hr Total Time: 1hr 10 mins Serves: 4 to 6

Ingredients:
- Broiled Garlic*
- 1 entire garlic bulb
- Additional virgin olive oil, for showering
- Ocean salt
- Pureed potatoes
- 2 pounds Yukon gold or tubby potatoes, stripped
- 2 teaspoons ocean salt, separated
- ⅓ cup extra-virgin olive oil
- Newly ground dark pepper
- Spread, optional for serving
- Chopped chives as well as rosemary, optional for sprinkling

Guidelines:
1. Preheat the oven to 350°F.

2. Make the simmered garlic: Trim the top ¼ inch off the highest point of the garlic bulb. Spot cut-side up on a piece of foil, shower with olive oil, and sprinkle with salt. Envelop the garlic by the foil and dish for 40 to an hour or until the cloves are profoundly golden brown and delicate. Eliminate from the oven and let cool somewhat. Utilize the rear of a gourmet specialist's blade or a little masher to pound the garlic into a paste prior to fusing into the pureed potatoes. Put away.
3. Make the pureed potatoes: Place the potatoes and 1 teaspoon of salt in a large pot and load up with enough water to cover the potatoes by 1 inch. Heat to the point of boiling and cook until fork delicate, around 20 minutes. Channel, saving 1 cup of the cooking fluid.
4. Utilize a ricer or a potato masher to squash the potatoes into a large bowl. Utilize an elastic spatula to crease in the simmered garlic, olive oil, ½ cup of the saved cooking fluid, 1 teaspoon salt, and a few portions of pepper. Keep collapsing until velvety, amounting to ½ cup seriously cooking fluid whenever wanted for creamier potatoes. Serve hot with spread, rosemary, and chives, whenever wanted.

Notes:
*Note: the simmered garlic can be made as long as 3 days ahead of time and put away in the refrigerator until prepared to utilize.

16. Farro

Prep Time: 5 mins Cook Time: 25 mins Total Time: 30 mins Serves: 4

Ingredients:

For the Farro:

- 1 cup uncooked farro, washed
- Lemon Herb Dressing:
- 1 tablespoon extra-virgin olive oil
- 1/2 tablespoon lemon juice, more to taste
- 1/2 tablespoon new thyme leaves
- 1 garlic clove, ground
- ¼ teaspoon Dijon mustard
- ½ teaspoon ocean salt, more to taste
- Newly ground dark pepper
- ½ cup chopped parsley
- touch of red pepper drops, optional

Directions:

1. Cook the farro: Fill a medium pot half loaded with water and heat to the point of boiling. Add the farro, lessen the heat and stew until the farro is delicate, chewy, yet at the same time has a still somewhat firm nibble - 15 to 20 minutes for pearled farro; 20 to 30 minutes for

semi-pearled farro; as long as 40 minutes for entire farro.

2. Channel, at that point spread onto a large plate or sheet skillet to cool and dry for 20 minutes. This holds it back from proceeding to steam which makes it soft.
3. Make the lemon spice dressing: Mixing the olive oil, lemon juice, thyme, garlic, mustard, salt, and pepper in the lower part of a large blending bowl. Add the farro and throw. Mix in the parsley and red pepper pieces, if using. Season to taste and serve.

NOTES:

Store cooked farro in the cooler for as long as 5 days. To freeze farro, first freeze it on a solitary layer on a preparing sheet, at that point move to a cooler holder.

Farro Tips:

1. Understand what sort of farro you have. Supermarkets commonly sell 3 sorts of farro: pearled, semi-pearled, and entirety. The cooking times for each change broadly, going from 15 minutes for pearled to 40 minutes for entirety. At the point when you purchase your farro, ensure you understand what kind you have – you don't need it to come out excessively hard or excessively soft! On the off chance that you don't have the foggiest idea what type you have – begin tasting it for doneness at 15 the moment mark and go from that point.

2. Group cook and freeze. Having a reserve of cooked grains close by is a lifeline with regards to feast preparing lunch or preparing a fast supper. Cooked farro keeps in the ice chest for 5 days, however you can freeze it for significantly more. To freeze it, spread the grains in a solitary layer on a heating sheet, and move it to the cooler for in any event 2 hours. After the grains are frozen, you can store them in a cooler safe holder. Try not to avoid the underlying hold up on the preparing sheet, or the grains will hold up in one major cluster!

3. Dress just prior to serving. I love to throw my farro with anything from a lemon vinaigrette (see the formula underneath) to cilantro lime dressing or chimichurri. On the off chance that you intend to dress yours, do it just prior to serving, as the kind of dressed grains blurs in the ice chest. However, in the event that you end up with extras, not to stress! Simply give them an additional press of lemon or lime and a sprinkle of salt and pepper prior to serving.

17. Roasted Beets

Prep Time: 15 mins Cook Time: 45 mins Total Time: 1hr Serves 4 as a side

Ingredients:

- 6 to 8 little or medium red or yellow beets
- Extra-virgin olive oil, for sprinkling
- 1 large navel orange
- Sherry vinegar or balsamic vinegar, for sprinkling
- Juice of ½ lemon, or to taste
- Modest bunch of watercress leaves, or arugula or microgreens
- Ocean salt and newly ground dark pepper
- Flaky ocean salt, optional
- other extra (optional) besting thoughts:
- Goat or feta cheddar
- Chopped pecans or pistachios

Directions:

1. Preheat the oven to 400°F.
2. Spot every beet on a piece of foil and shower liberally with olive oil and portions of ocean salt and newly ground dark pepper. Enclose the

beets by the foil and dish on a preparing sheet for 35 to an hour, or until delicate and fork-delicate. The time will rely upon the size and newness of the beets. Eliminate the beets from the oven, eliminate the foil, and put away to cool. At the point when they are cool to the touch, strip the skins. I like to hold them under running water and slide the skins off with my mind.

3. Utilize a citrus peeler to strip long strips around the orange, staying away from the white essence. Ground zing would work here moreover. Cut ¾ of the orange into portions and hold the excess ¼ wedge for pressing.

4. Cut the beets into 1" wedges or pieces and spot them in a bowl. In case you're using red and yellow beets, place each tone into independent dishes so the red beets don't stain the yellow beets.

5. Sprinkle with olive oil and sherry vinegar, at that point add the lemon juice, squeezed orange pressed from the leftover wedge, and a couple of portions of salt and pepper and throw. Chill until prepared to serve.

6. Taste prior to serving and season with more salt (flaky ocean salt, if using) and pepper or more vinegar (for more tang), orange, or lemon juice, as wanted.

7. Serve on a platter with the orange fragments, watercress, and citrus twists.

8. Simmered Beets Recipe Variations

9. Top it with squashed, toasted pistachios or pecans for crunch.

10. Sprinkle it with tart feta or goat cheddar.

11. Add broiled chickpeas, quinoa, farro, or wheat berries to make it heartier.
12. Trimming the last dish with thyme leaves or chopped parsley.
13. Avoid the watercress, and make a serving of mixed greens! Cleave the beets and serve them on a bed of spinach.
14. Change the marinade! Throw the simmered beets with apple juice vinegar dressing or lemon vinaigrette.
15. Tell me what varieties you attempt!
16. Simmered Beets Serving Suggestions
17. This simmered beets formula is a delectable supper side dish. Serve it with your #1 protein or a generous pasta like my mushroom pasta, sun-dried tomato pasta, butternut squash ravioli, or spaghetti aglio e olio.
18. It would likewise be an extraordinary expansion to a Thanksgiving or occasion menu, served close by exemplary dishes like these.

18. Kale Pesto Mushroom Pistachio Bowls

Serves: 2-3
Ingredients:
Kale Pesto Sauce:

- ¼ cup Southern Grove Pistachios, shelled
- 1 garlic clove
- 1 pressed cup SimplyNature Organic Chopped Kale
- 2 tablespoons new lemon juice
- ¼ teaspoon salt
- Newly ground dark pepper
- ¼ cup Specially Selected Premium Italian Extra Virgin Olive Oil
- ¼ cup water

For the Bowls:

- 1 tablespoon SimplyNature Organic Extra Virgin Olive Oil

- 16 ounces Baby Bella mushrooms, cut
- 2 teaspoons Simply Nature Aged Balsamic Dressing
- 4 stuffed cups Simply Nature Organic Chopped Kale
- 2 cups cooked Simply Nature Organic Quinoa
- ½ cup Dakota's Pride Garbanzo Beans, washed and depleted
- 1 tablespoon squashed Southern Grove Pistachios
- Portions of Stone mill Crushed Red Pepper, optional
- ¼ teaspoon ocean salt, more to taste
- Newly ground dark pepper

Guidelines:
Join the pistachios, garlic, kale, lemon juice, ocean salt, pepper, ¼ cup olive oil and ¼ cup water in a little blender and heartbeat until pureed.

Heat the oil in a large skillet over medium heat. Add the mushrooms, ¼ teaspoon ocean salt, pepper, mix to cover, at that point cook 8 to 10 minutes or until the mushrooms are browned and softened, mixing sporadically. Eliminate from heat and throw with the balsamic.

In a medium bowl, finely hack the excess kale and eliminate any intense stem pieces. Throw with a couple of scoops of the kale pesto sauce and season with salt and pepper. Throw and delicately rub.

Amass the dishes with the cooked quinoa, kale, mushrooms, chickpeas, pistachios, red pepper pieces and liberal scoops of the sauce. Season to taste.

19. Macro Veggie Bowl

Prep Time: 20 minsCook Time: 20 mins Serves 4

Ingredients:
- 1 watermelon radish or 2 red radishes
- press of lemon
- 1 uncooked cup grew mung beans or cooked lentils
- 6 little or 3 medium carrots, steamed
- 1 little head broccoli florets, steamed
- 8 kale leaves, chopped
- 2 cups brown rice or quinoa
- ¾ cup sauerkraut or other aged veggie
- 2 tablespoons sesame seeds or hemp seeds
- microgreens, optional
- Ocean salt and newly broke dark pepper
- Turmeric Tahini
- 1 tablespoon extra-virgin olive oil
- 1 tablespoon lemon juice
- 1/2 tablespoon tahini
- 1/2 tablespoon water
- 1/2 garlic clove, minced
- 1/4 teaspoon ground turmeric

- ocean salt and newly broke dark pepper

Directions:

1. Make the sauce. In a little bowl, combine as one the olive oil, lemon juice, tahini, water, garlic, turmeric, and liberal portions of salt and pepper. Put away.
2. Daintily cut the radish (this is best done on a mandolin), and throw the cuts with a crush of lemon. Put away.
3. Cook the mung beans in bubbling salted water as per bundle directions, or until delicate. Channel.
4. In a liner bushel over a pot of stewing water, steam the carrots, covered, until simply delicate, 7 to 10 minutes. Eliminate and put away. Next steam the broccoli until delicate yet at the same time dazzling green, 4 to 5 minutes. In conclusion, steam the kale until simply delicate, 30 seconds to 1 moment.
5. Gather singular dishes with the brown rice, mung beans, carrots, broccoli, kale, sauerkraut, sesame seeds and microgreens, if using. Season with salt and pepper and present with the Turmeric Tahini Sauce.
6. Veggie Bowl Recipe Variations
7. This formula is phenomenal as-composed, however go ahead and switch things up! Here are a couple of thoughts to kick you off:
8. Cook the veggies in an alternate manner. Rather than steaming the broccoli, cook it!

You could likewise cook the carrots or depart the kale crude and back rub it prior to adding it to your bowl.

9. Or then again utilize various veggies altogether. Cooked vegetables like cauliflower, yams, butternut squash, Brussels fledglings, and beets would all be extraordinary increments to this formula.

10. Trade in an alternate vegetable. I suggest dark beans, lentils, or broiled chickpeas, yet an alternate protein, as prepared tofu or tempeh, would work here, as well.

11. Fluctuate your grain. Trade the brown rice for quinoa, farro, or white rice. Or on the other hand, for additional veggie power, go sans grain and use cauliflower rice!

12. Switch the sauce. Truly, your choices are perpetual. Attempt one of these 4 tahini sauce varieties or this tahini dressing. You could likewise sprinkle on green goddess dressing, veggie lover farm, cilantro lime dressing, or the carrot ginger dressing from this formula!

20. Rainbow Bowls w/ Almond-Ginger Dressing

Prep time: 20 min Serves: serves 4

Ingredients:

- 1 red pepper, daintily cut
- 1 large cucumber, spiralized or daintily cut
- 1 large carrot, stripped into strips
- 1 cup split cherry tomatoes, any tone or assortment
- 6 cups free stuffed delicate child kale or spinach
- 2 cups shredded purple cabbage
- 8 to 10 basil leaves, chopped
- 2 scallions, chopped
- ½ cup edamame or protein of decision
- 2 tablespoons hemp seeds

- 8 ounces cooked brown rice noodles (more in the event that you like a higher noodle proportion)
- Almond-Ginger Dressing
- ¼ cup almond or cashew spread
- ¼ cup new lime juice
- 1½ tablespoons tamari, in addition to additional to taste
- 1 garlic clove, minced
- ½ teaspoon minced ginger
- ⅓ cup Almond Breeze Almondmilk Cashewmilk Original
- optional: a spurt of sriracha

Directions:

1. Make the dressing: In a little bowl, consolidate the almond margarine, lime juice, tamari, ginger and garlic. Speed until smooth. Add the Almond Cashewmilk and race to consolidate. (Now, the dressing may taste somewhat pungent and solid yet whenever it's thrown with the entirety of the vegetables, the flavors will turn out to be more adjusted). Chill until prepared to utilize. In the event that it isolates, give it a little mix prior to using.
2. In an extremely large bowl, join the pepper, cucumber, carrot, cherry tomatoes, kale, cabbage, basil, scallions, edamame, hemp seeds and brown rice noodles. Add the dressing and throw well so the vegetables start to shrink. Taste and season with more tamari, whenever wanted.

21. Sweet Potato Noodles with Garlic & Kale

Serves: *4 as a side, 3 as a fundamental*

Ingredients:

- 2 medium yams, spiralized
- 1 to 2 tablespoons extra-virgin olive oil, enough to well cover the skillet
- 3 garlic cloves, meagerly cut
- ¼ teaspoon red pepper drops, more as wanted
- 2 to 3 tablespoons water
- 4 cups infant kale (or meagerly cut lacinato kale)
- ocean salt and newly ground dark pepper
- crushes of new lemon juice, as wanted
- present with:
- ⅓ cup new basil, cut
- touches of pesto (this formula with basil instead of kale)
- 2 tablespoons hemp seeds or toasted pine nuts
- ground pecorino cheddar, optional

Directions:

1. Strip the yams. Cut down the middle and cut the sharp warns. Spot in the spiralizer and spiralize into noodles. On the other hand, you can utilize a julienne peeler (albeit this is more troublesome, so I suggest spiralizing).
2. Heat the oil in a large profound skillet over medium heat. Add the garlic and cook until the garlic cuts are delicately golden brown, around 5 minutes, decreasing the heat if important (ie, if the olive oil is foaming excessively, turn the heat down, you don't need the garlic to consume). Add a couple of liberal portions of salt, red pepper pieces, and a couple of toils of newly broke dark pepper.
3. Add the yam noodles and throw to cover. Let cook for 2 minutes, delicately throwing and scratching down the sides of the container.
4. Add 2 to 3 tablespoons of water and throw again to guarantee that nothing is adhering to the lower part of the dish. Cover and let the yam noodles proceed for 5 additional minutes or until they begin to relax and are delicate yet at the same time suffer a heart attack "still somewhat firm" chomp. Check and throw every so often with the goal that they cook equally. Be mindful so as not to overcook or they will begin to fall to pieces (this happens rapidly).
5. During the last moment of cooking, mix in the kale so it shrivels into the noodles. Eliminate from heat and move to 3 or 4 dishes.
6. Present with the new basil, a bit of pesto, hemp seeds or pine nuts and pecorino cheddar, whenever wanted.

Notes:
On the off chance that you don't suffer a heart attack, this formula would likewise be delightful with spaghetti squash rather than the yam. Add pre-simmered spaghetti squash in sync 3, and afterward skip stage 4 - the spaghetti squash won't require the additional water or the additional cook time.

22. Sun Dried Tomato Pasta with Kale

Prep time: 10 mins Cook time: 20 mins Total time: 30 mins Serves: 4

Ingredients:

- 2 tablespoons extra-virgin olive oil, more for showering
- 3 shallots, daintily cut
- 1 large fennel bulb, daintily cut
- 3 garlic cloves, cut
- ¼ teaspoon red pepper chips
- ¼ cup chopped sage
- 12-ounces toscani pasta (or any short pasta)
- ¼ cup dry white wine
- 8 cups torn kale leaves
- 8 oil-stuffed sun-dried tomatoes, chopped
- ¼ cup chopped pecans, toasted
- 2 tablespoons new lemon juice
- Ocean salt and newly ground dark pepper
- Newly ground pecorino cheddar, for serving

Directions:

1. Heat the oil in a large skillet over medium heat. Add the shallots, fennel, garlic, red pepper pieces, sage, ½ teaspoon salt, and newly ground dark pepper and cook until the fennel is delicate, around 8 minutes.
2. In the mean time, heat a large pot of salted water to the point of boiling and cook the pasta until still somewhat firm.
3. To the skillet, add the white wine and let it diminish for 30 seconds. At that point, diminish the heat to low, add the kale and throw until just withered. Utilize an opened spoon to scoop the cooked pasta into the skillet. Add the sun-dried tomatoes, pecans, and lemon squeeze and throw.
4. At last, season to taste and present with liberal sprinkles of olive oil and newly ground pecorino cheddar.

Notes:
Make this gluten free by using gluten free pasta.

23. Spaghetti Aglio e Olio

Prep Time: 5 mins Cook Time: 15 mins Total Time: 20 mins Serves 4

Ingredients:

- 12 ounces spaghetti
- ½ to 1 cup pasta water
- ¼ cup extra-virgin olive oil
- 4 garlic cloves, daintily cut
- ¼ to ½ teaspoon red pepper chips
- 1 large pack lacinato kale, stemmed and chopped
- ½ teaspoon ocean salt
- Newly ground dark pepper
- 1 teaspoon lemon zing
- 1 teaspoon lemon juice
- ⅓ cup chopped parsley
- Parmesan or Vegan Parmesan, for serving

Directions:

1. Set up the pasta as per the bundle directions, in a pot of salted bubbling water, until still somewhat firm. Save 1 cup of the pasta cooking water prior to depleting the pasta.
2. Heat the oil in a large skillet over medium heat. Add the garlic and red pepper chips. Mix and cook 30 seconds to 1 moment, until the garlic is delicately browned around the edges. Add the kale, salt, and a few drudgeries of pepper and cook, throwing with utensils, until the kale is withered, as long as 1 moment.
3. Add the spaghetti and throw to join. Add ½ cup pasta water, lemon juice, lemon zing, and throw. In the event that the pasta is appearing to be excessively dry, add the leftover ½ cup pasta water to make a light sauce.
4. Season to taste. Enhancement with parsley and present with Parmesan or vegetarian Parmesan.

24. Alkaline kale salad

Prep Time: 15 mins Cook Time: 25 mins Total Time: 40 mins Serves: 4

Ingredients:

- Carrot Ginger Dressing (see note)
- ½ cup chopped cooked carrots, from 3/4 cup crude carrots
- 1/3 to ½ cup water
- ¼ cup extra-virgin olive oil
- 2 tablespoons rice vinegar
- 2 teaspoons minced ginger
- ¼ teaspoon ocean salt
- Salad
- 1 clump Roasted Chickpeas
- 1 bundle wavy kale, stems eliminated, leaves torn
- 1 teaspoon lemon juice
- ½ teaspoon extra-virgin olive oil
- 1 little carrot, ground
- 1 little red beet, grated*
- ½ watermelon radish, meagerly cut
- 1 avocado, cubed

- 2 tablespoons dried cranberries
- ¼ cup pepitas, toasted
- 1 teaspoon sesame seeds
- Ocean salt and Freshly ground dark pepper

Guidelines:

1. Make the dressing and dish the chickpeas: Preheat the oven to 400°F and fix a large preparing sheet with material paper. Throw the chickpeas with a shower of olive oil and sprinkle with portions of salt and pepper. Spot the carrot pieces for the dressing in their own corner on the preparing sheet to broil close by the chickpeas. Cook for 25 to minutes, or until the chickpeas are browned and fresh and the carrots are delicate. Put the simmered chickpeas away. Move the carrots to a blender and add the water, olive oil, rice vinegar, ginger, and salt. Mix the dressing until smooth and chill in the cooler until prepared to utilize.

2. Spot the kale leaves into a large bowl and shower with the lemon juice, ½ teaspoon of olive oil, and a couple of portions of salt. Utilize your hands to knead the leaves until they become delicate and withered and lessen in the bowl by about half.

3. Add the carrot, beet, watermelon radish, half of the cubed avocado, cranberries, pepitas, a couple of all the more great portions of salt and a couple of toils of pepper, and throw. Shower liberally with the carrot ginger dressing. Top with the excess avocado, really dressing, the simmered chickpeas and sprinkle

with the sesame seeds. Season to taste and serve.

Notes:
Make the dressing ahead so it has the opportunity to chill in the cooler prior to adding to the plate of mixed greens.

25. Ribollita –

Prep time: 10 mins Cook time: 50 mins Total time:
1hour Serves: 2-3
Ingredients:

- 2 tablespoons extra-virgin olive oil
- 1 little onion, chopped
- 3 carrots, chopped
- 1 tablespoon finely chopped rosemary
- 2 garlic cloves, minced
- 3 medium Roma or plant tomatoes, diced
- ½ teaspoon red pepper chips
- 2 tablespoons white wine
- 1½ cups cooked cannellini beans, depleted and washed
- 4 cups vegetable stock
- 3 large lacinato kale leaves, daintily cut, coarse stems eliminated
- 4 thick cuts flat crusty bread, cubed
- balsamic vinegar, for showering
- ¼ cup shaved Parmesan cheddar, optional
- ocean salt and newly ground dark pepper

Directions:

1. Heat the olive oil in a large pot over medium heat. Add the onion and portions of salt and pepper and cook, mixing infrequently, until the onion is delicate, around 4 minutes. Mix in the carrots, rosemary, and garlic. Cook for around 4 additional minutes, diminishing the heat if important to try not to consume the garlic.
2. Add the tomatoes, red pepper chips, and another couple of portions of salt and pepper. Cook, blending frequently, for around 15 minutes or until the tomatoes are delicate and delicious. Add the wine and let it cook off, around 1 moment.
3. Mix in the beans, and afterward add the vegetable stock. Stew until the carrots are delicate, 30 to 35 minutes, blending sometimes.
4. When the carrots are delicate, mix in the kale, the cubed bread, and a sprinkle of balsamic vinegar. Stew for a few additional minutes until the kale is shriveled.
5. Season to taste and serve hot in large dishes. Shave new Parmesan cheddar on top, whenever wanted.

Notes:

Twofold this formula to make a larger clump. Store extras in the cooler for as long as two days.
New tomatoes can be fill in for around 1 cup of canned diced tomatoes.

Conclusion

I would like to thank you for picking this book. It contains recipes which are according to alkaline diet schedule and incorporate many health benefits. Try at home and enjoy.

THE ESSENTIAL ALKALINE COOKBOOK FOR BEGINNERS

Table of Contents

INTRODUCTION

The main factor in the alkaline diet is balance. In sound people, a diet of 65% (by weight) alkaline-framing food varieties and 35% corrosive shaping functions admirably. For instance, if you somehow managed to have a 8-ounce steak for supper, you'd need to eat around 23 ounces of alkaline-shaping food sources during the day to keep up the 65-35 proportion. In those with wellbeing challenges, a 80-20 proportion of alkaline-shaping to corrosive framing food varieties is proposed, basically on the grounds that it lessens the measure of exertion your body needs to place into diminishing its corrosive burden. (This means 40 ounces of alkaline-shaping food varieties as remuneration for your 8-ounce steak — or you could basically scale your steak back to 4 ounces all things being equal.).

In spite of the fact that blood pH should remain stable in a thin scope of 7.35–7.45 for endurance, the equivalent isn't valid for the pH of different liquids like pee and salivation, as these will shift for the duration of the day. The pH of the pee goes all over as indicated by the food sources we eat, exercise, stress, and different factors. The kidney is the essential organ answerable for buffering and discharging metabolic acids, however the kidney can't discharge pee that is more acidic than a pH of 4.5, as pee this corrosive would copy the sensitive tissues of the kidney. Strangely, in the event that you eat an exceptionally corrosive framing supper, your pee will regularly show an alkaline pH a couple of hours after the fact. You may think this means that great foundational pH balance; nonetheless, this is the impact of the pancreas creating high measures of alkalizing stomach related mixtures because of the corrosive shaping food varieties ingested.

On the off chance that you are keen on estimating corrosive burden through a pee pH perusing, the most precise measure is with the principal morning pee following 6 hours of rest. On the off chance that you can't go six hours without getting up to pee, simply measure your first-morning pee when you get up for the afternoon, however don't gobble or work when you get up to pee in the evening.

26. Vegan Stuffing

Prep Time: 15 minsCook Time: 40 minsTotal Time: 55 mins
Serves 8

Ingredients

- 6 tablespoons extra-virgin olive oil, separated
- 1 cup coarsely chopped cipollini onions
- 3 cups chopped and stemmed mushrooms, blend of shiitakes and creminis
- 3 garlic cloves, minced
- 2 stems celery, diced
- 1/4 cup chopped wise, in addition to 8 leaves for decorate
- 2 tablespoons minced rosemary

- 2 tablespoons balsamic vinegar
- 5 cups cubed hard crusty bread + nine-grain bread*
- 3 lacinato kale leaves, coarsely chopped or torn
- 2 cups vegetable stock, in addition to additional for reheating
- 1/4 cup dried cranberries
- Ocean salt and newly ground dark pepper

Directions:
1. Preheat the oven to 350°F and oil a 8x12 or 9x13 meal dish.
2. In an exceptionally enormous skillet, heat 2 tablespoons of the olive oil over medium heat. Add the onions, mushrooms, 1/2 teaspoon salt, and a few toils of new pepper, and let the mushrooms cook until they start to relax, 5 to 8 minutes, blending just periodically. Add the garlic, celery, sage, and rosemary, and cook until everything is delicate and the mushrooms are brilliant brown, 8-10 minutes.
3. Add the balsamic vinegar, mix, and scratch any pieces off the lower part of the skillet. Add the bread and the excess 1/4 cup olive oil and throw to cover. Add the kale and cook until it starts to shrink, around 1 moment. Add 1 cup of the stock and mix.
4. Move to a meal dish and pour the leftover 1 cup stock equally absurd.
5. Sprinkle with the dried cranberries, staying entire sage leaves and prepare for 20 minutes or until brilliant brown. Let sit for in any event 15 minutes or until prepared to serve.

6. Notes

7. To reheat, add a smidgen more stock and heat until warmed through and marginally fresh on top.
8. *Crusty pastry kitchen bread works best in this formula. Delicate sandwich bread will turn out to be excessively spongy.
9. Vegetarian Stuffing Recipe Tips
10. Trade the mushrooms. While I love the exquisite kind of the shiitakes in this stuffing formula, it's likewise heavenly with various mushroom assortments. Take a stab at making it with cremini mushrooms, or with a blend of shiitakes and creminis.
11. Utilize your number one bread. I call for crusty bread and nine grain bread in this formula, yet it works similarly too with any great dry bread. French or sourdough bread would both be astounding. Also, in the event that you need to make your stuffing without gluten, sub in the best portion of without gluten bread you can discover!
12. Purchase (or make!) your bread a day early. In the event that you've never made stuffing without any preparation, you may be amazed to discover that using dried bread will really improve it! Dry, day-old bread blocks will absorb the olive oil, stock, and mushroom juices like a wipe, which makes for extra-delectable stuffing.
13. Make it ahead of time. Like any extraordinary Thanksgiving side dish, this veggie lover stuffing formula is far superior in the event that you make it early. I like it more the more it

sits, it's as yet scrumptious on the subsequent day! To reheat it, add some additional stock and heat at 350° until it's warmed through and softly fresh on top.

27. Cranberry Sauce

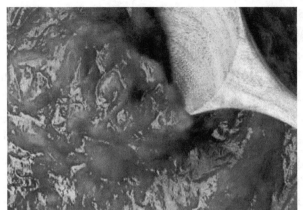

Prep Time: 5 minsCook Time: 20 mins
Serves 8
Ingredients
- 4 cups new cranberries
- ½ cup maple syrup
- ¼ cup water
- 1 teaspoon orange zing
- Touch of salt
- Directions

Strategy:
1. In a medium pot over medium-low heat, consolidate the cranberries, maple syrup, water, orange zing, and salt. Bring to a stew, blending frequently so the maple syrup doesn't consume.
2. Decrease the heat to low and cook, mixing regularly, until the cranberries burst and the sauce has thickened, 15 to 20 minutes. Taste and change the flavors, whenever wanted, and serve.
3. Custom made Cranberry Sauce Recipe Tips

4. Cook it how you like it. Hand crafted cranberry sauce thickens as it cools, so keep that it mind as you make this formula. Quit cooking when the sauce is somewhat more slender than you'd like it to be. I like my sauce to be genuinely thick, with a blend of entire and burst berries, so I cook it for around 18 minutes. On the off chance that you like your sauce to be more slender, or to have all the more entire berries, cook it for less time, around 12 to 15 minutes.

5. Taste and change. Try to taste this cranberry sauce before you serve it. I like mine overall quite tart, yet in the event that you favor a better or zestier cranberry sauce, go ahead and change it! Add extra maple to make your sauce better, or mix in additional orange zing for a more grounded orange flavor.

6. Make it ahead of time. This natively constructed cranberry sauce keeps well in a sealed shut compartment in the ice chest for as long as 4 days. In the event that you make it early, permit it to come to room temperature prior to serving.

7. Save the extras! Have a little sauce extra from a vacation feast? Try not to allow it to go to squander! Consider the extra sauce a thick, tart jam. Spot it onto oats or overnight oats, top it onto flapjacks or French toast, or spread it onto a sweet and flavorful pre-winter sandwich. On the off chance that you have additional serving thoughts, let me know in the remarks!

28. Mushroom Gravy

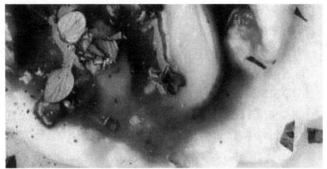

***Prep Time: 15 mins Cook Time: 30 mins
Serves 8***

Ingredients:
- 2 tablespoons extra-virgin olive oil
- 1 shallot, finely chopped (⅓ cup)
- 16 ounces cremini mushrooms, cut
- ½ tablespoon tamari
- 2 garlic cloves, minced
- 1½ tablespoons new thyme leaves
- ½ tablespoon chopped rosemary
- ¼ cup generally useful flour
- 3 cups vegetable stock
- Ocean salt and newly ground dark pepper

Guidelines:
1. Heat the olive oil in a huge skillet over medium heat. Add the shallot and cook until delicate, around 4 minutes.
2. Add the mushrooms and cook until delicate, around 8 to 10 minutes. Mix in the tamari, garlic, thyme, and rosemary. Sprinkle the flour over the mushrooms and mix for 1 moment.

3. Add the stock and stew until thickened, whisking frequently, around 20 minutes. Season with salt and pepper to taste.
4. **Notes:**
5. Make this formula gluten free: Omit the flour in sync 2. Toward the finish of stage 3, spoon a couple of tablespoons of the fluid into a little bowl. Add 2 tablespoons cornstarch and mix until smooth. Empty this blend once more into the container and mix until the sauce thickens.
6. Mushroom Gravy Serving Suggestions
7. This mushroom sauce would be a tasty expansion to a Thanksgiving or occasion supper. I love it with exemplary side dishes like stuffing and simmered Brussels sprouts, however like any great sauce formula, it's best with pureed potatoes. Spoon it over my conventional broiled garlic pureed potatoes, or attempt an out-of-the-case crush all things being equal. This vegetarian mushroom sauce would be an ideal fixing for my pounded cauliflower or parsnip puree.
8. In the event that you have any extras, mix some cooked white beans into the sauce, pour it over velvety pounded cauliflower, and enjoy it as a supper all alone! Indeed, I like this blend such a lot of that I make it for supper all through the fall and winter. Presented with custom made focaccia or dried up bread, it's fantastic, sound, and ameliorating.

29. Sweet Potato Casserole

Prep Time: 20 mins Cook Time: 1hr 20 mins
Total Time: 1hr 40 mins Serves 6 to 8

Ingredients

- 5 huge yams
- 1 tablespoon extra-virgin olive oil, more for showering
- 1/4 cup almond milk, more if fundamental
- 1 teaspoon ground ginger
- ½ teaspoon ocean salt
- 1/8 teaspoon dark pepper
- ½ cup new sage leaves
- Disintegrate Topping
- ⅓ cup entire moved oats
- ¼ cup walnuts, more for embellish
- ¼ cup pecans, more for embellish
- ½ garlic clove
- 2 teaspoons maple syrup
- 1 tablespoon extra-virgin olive oil
- ¼ teaspoon dried thyme leaves
- ¼ teaspoon minced new rosemary
- 1 teaspoon ocean salt

- 1/8 teaspoon dark pepper

Directions :

1. Preheat the oven to 425°F. Line a preparing sheet with foil and brush a 8x11-inch heating dish, or comparable, with olive oil.
2. Utilize a fork to punch a couple of holes into the yams. Spot on the preparing sheet and dish until exceptionally delicate, around an hour.
3. Make the disintegrate beating: In a food processor, place the oats, walnuts, pecans, garlic, maple syrup, olive oil, thyme, rosemary, and salt and heartbeat until just consolidated. Eliminate and put away.
4. Scoop the cooked yam tissue out of the skins and spot in a food processor. Add the olive oil, almond milk, ginger, salt, and a few drudgeries of pepper and interaction to consolidate. Spread the combination into the heating dish.
5. Sprinkle with the disintegrate beating, extra nuts, and sage. Shower with olive oil and heat 20 minutes or until the fixing is browned and fresh.
6. Yam Casserole Recipe Tips
7. Heat your yams until they're really delicate. You need the filling of this meal to be delicious and rich, with no lumps. Ensure that a fork can without much of a stretch slide through the potatoes when you remove them from the oven. Thusly, they'll mix into a totally smooth puree.
8. Save some entire nuts for embellish! The best chomps of this dish join velvety yam with

enormous, hot nuts. At the point when you mix up disintegrate, save a couple of entire nuts to dab on top. You'll say thanks to yourself later.

9. Make it ahead. Like all incredible Thanksgiving recipes, this sound yam dish is not difficult to prepare early. You can do nearly everything daily or two preceding your banquet: mix up the yam filling, beat together the disintegrate garnish, and store them in isolated holders in the refrigerator. Just prior to serving, sprinkle disintegrate over the filling, and heat! (In the event that you prepare the whole dish early, the garnish will lose its freshness in the cooler.)

30. Kale & Olive Oil Vegan Mashed Potatoes

Cook time 20 mins Total time20 mins Serves: 4 to 6

Ingredients

- 2 pounds unpeeled yellow potatoes (or Yukon Gold), cut into 1 inch pieces
- 4 garlic cloves, stripped
- ⅓ cup extra-virgin olive oil, more for sprinkling
- ¼ cup chopped scallions
- 4 cups finely chopped kale (1 little pack)
- 2 tablespoons minced new rosemary
- Ocean salt and newly ground dark pepper
- Portions of red pepper drops (optional)

Guidelines:

1. Spot the potatoes, garlic, and 1 teaspoon salt in an enormous pot and load up with enough water to cover the potatoes by 1 inch. Heat to the point of boiling and cook until fork delicate,

around 15 minutes. Channel, saving 1 cup of the cooking fluid.

2. Heat ½ teaspoon olive oil in a medium skillet. Add the scallions and kale, and cook until withered, 1 to 2 minutes. Put away.

3. Utilize a potato masher to coarsely pound the potatoes and garlic. Utilize an elastic spatula to overlap in the ⅓ cup olive oil, ½ cup of the held cooking fluid, the kale, scallions, rosemary, ½ teaspoon salt and newly ground dark pepper. Keep collapsing until smooth, amounting to ½ cup seriously cooking fluid and extra sprinkles of olive oil, whenever wanted. Season to taste with up to ½ teaspoon more salt, and portions of red pepper chips, whenever wanted. Serve hot.

31. Parsnip Puree

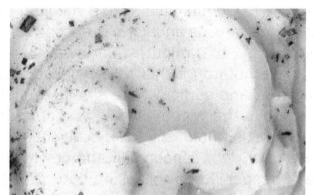

Prep Time: 10 mins Cook Time: 40 mins Total Time: 50 mins Serves 6 to 8 as a side

Main ingredients:

- Parsnips! On the off chance that you've never cooked with parsnips, you're in for a treat. They suffer a heart attack, complex flavor that makes this puree truly novel.
- Cauliflower – Many parsnip puree recipes call for cream or margarine, however mixed cauliflower supplies a similar rich, tasty surface. It's such a great deal better, as well!
- Broiled garlic – It lifts the nutty kind of the parsnips.
- Lemon juice – For brilliance.
- New rosemary – It adds hearty, comfortable fall flavor.
- Olive oil – It adds sufficient wealth to make this unequivocally solid dish taste the perfect measure of unfortunate. Yum!

Ingredients:

- 5 medium parsnips (1 pound), stripped and chopped into 1-inch pieces

- 1 medium cauliflower (2 pounds), broken into pieces, including the centers
- 5 cloves Roasted Garlic
- 2 tablespoons extra-virgin olive oil, more for sprinkling
- ½ tablespoon new lemon juice
- ½ to 1 teaspoon ocean salt
- 1 loading teaspoon minced rosemary
- Newly ground dark pepper, to taste

Directions:
1. Tip: broil the garlic ahead of time and store any additional cloves in the cooler.
2. Heat a huge pot of salted water to the point of boiling and heat up the parsnips and cauliflower for 10 to 12 minutes or until fork delicate. Move to a blender.
3. Add the broiled garlic to the blender alongside the olive oil, lemon juice, ½ teaspoon of salt, and a touch of pepper. Mix, using the blender stick to push down the substance, and mix to a smooth consistency. On the off chance that essential, add a touch of water or stock to get the blender rolling, however do so sparingly so the puree doesn't turn out to be excessively slight. Taste and add the extra ½ teaspoon of salt, whenever wanted.
4. Move to a serving bowl and mix in the rosemary while the crush is still warm. Add a sprinkle of olive oil, more pepper, whenever wanted, and serve hot.

32. Garlic Mashed Cauliflower

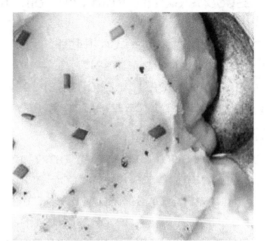

Total time: 30 min Cook time: 10 min Serves 3 to 4

Ingredients

- 1 medium head cauliflower, 2 pounds, chopped
- 2 tablespoons dissolved margarine or vegetarian spread
- 7 cloves simmered garlic
- ⅛ to ¼ teaspoon Dijon mustard
- ¼ to ½ teaspoon ocean salt
- Newly ground dark pepper
- Chives, for embellish, optional

Directions:

1. Heat a huge pot of salted water to the point of boiling. Add the cauliflower and bubble until blade delicate, around 10 minutes. Channel and move to a food processor.
2. Puree the cauliflower with the spread, garlic, mustard, salt, and pepper. Season to taste and enhancement with chives, whenever wanted.

3. Garlic Mashed Cauliflower Serving Suggestions
4. Like exemplary pureed potatoes, this crushed cauliflower would be an incredible expansion to alkaline diet or occasion feast. It reheats well, so make it as long as 2 days ahead of time and store it in the cooler. At the point when you eat, serve it close to conventional side dishes like green bean meal, yam goulash, and stuffing. Remember the pumpkin pie for dessert!
5. Recently, I've likewise been enjoying these cauliflower pureed potatoes as a dinner all alone. Finished off with mushroom sauce (search for the formula not long from now!) and cooked white beans for protein, they're the ideal fall solace food. I balance everything with a cooked veggie like butternut squash or broccoli and a cut of hard bread or hand crafted focaccia.

33. Roasted Delicata Squash with Apples

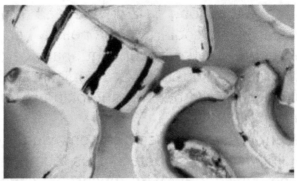

Prep Time: 20 mins Cook Time: 40 mins Total Time: 1hr Serves 4 as a side
Ingredients:
- 2 delicata squash, divided the long way and cultivated, cut into ½-inch pieces
- ½ cup pearl onions, divided
- Additional virgin olive oil, for sprinkling
- 2 tablespoons pepitas or potentially pine nuts
- 2 cups torn lacinato kale, 2 to 3 leaves
- 6 sage leaves, chopped
- Leaves from 3 thyme branches
- 1 little function apple, diced
- Ocean salt and newly ground dark pepper
- Dressing:
- 2 tablespoons extra-virgin olive oil
- 1 tablespoon apple juice vinegar
- ½ garlic clove, minced
- ¼ teaspoon Dijon mustard
- ⅛ teaspoon maple syrup
- ocean salt and newly ground dark pepper

Guidelines:

1. Preheat the oven to 425°F and fix a preparing sheet with material paper.
2. Spot the squash and onions on the preparing sheet and shower with olive oil and liberal portions of salt and pepper. Throw to cover and organize on the sheet so that they're not contacting. Broil until the squash is brilliant brown on all sides and until the onions are delicate and browned, 25 to 30 minutes.
3. Make the dressing: In a little bowl, whisk together the olive oil, apple juice vinegar, garlic, mustard, maple syrup, and a spot of salt and pepper. Put away.
4. In a little skillet over medium-low heat, throw the pepitas with a touch of salt and cook until toasted, mixing often, for around 2 minutes. Put away.
5. In a medium blending bowl, consolidate the kale, sage, and thyme. Add the warm cooked squash and onions, the apples, a large portion of the pepitas, and a large portion of the dressing. Throw to cover. Move to an oven-safe serving dish. (In case you're making this dish ahead of time stop here and follow the saving/reheating guidelines in the notes underneath).
6. Spot the serving dish into the oven for 8 to 10 minutes, or until the apples and kale are warm and the kale is simply shriveled. Not long prior to serving, shower with the excess dressing, and top with the leftover pepitas.
7. **Notes:**
8. Make-ahead directions: Once the broiled vegetables are moved to the serving dish, cool

to room temp. Cover with foil and chill the dish until prepared to reheat (Ideally, make this around 4 hours ahead of time). At the point when prepared to reheat, preheat the oven to 425°. Release the thwart and prepare, inexactly covered for 12 to 15 minutes or until everything is heated through. Not long prior to serving, shower with the leftover dressing, and top with the excess pepitas.

9. Broiled Delicata Squash Recipe Serving Suggestions

10. This formula is delectable hot from the oven, yet you can likewise prepare it a couple of hours ahead of time! (Discover the make-ahead guidelines in the formula beneath.) subsequently, it's an incredible possibility for an uncommon event dinner or Thanksgiving feast. It matches magnificently with other fall side dishes like green bean meal, pureed potatoes, and broiled Brussels sprouts. See this post for more most loved Thanksgiving recipes, and remember the pumpkin pie or apple disintegrate for dessert!

11. Obviously, this broiled delicata squash formula is a yummy expansion to an ordinary supper as well.

34. Many-Veggie Vegetable Soup

Prep Time: 10 mins Cook Time: 30 mins Total Time: 40 mins Serves 6

Ingredients:

- 2 tablespoons extra-virgin olive oil
- 1 medium yellow onion, diced
- Ocean salt and new dark pepper
- 1 medium carrot, diced
- 1 little yam, diced
- ¼ cup dry white wine, i.e., pinot grigio
- 1 14.5-ounce can diced fire broiled tomatoes
- 4 garlic cloves, chopped
- 2 teaspoons dried oregano, or 2 tablespoons chopped new thyme or rosemary
- ¼ teaspoon red pepper pieces, more to taste
- 4 cups vegetable stock
- 2 inlet leaves
- 1 cup split cherry tomatoes
- 1 cup chopped green beans
- 1 zucchini, diced
- 1 15-ounce can chickpeas, depleted and washed
- 2 tablespoons white wine vinegar
- 1½ cups chopped kale

Directions:

1. Heat the oil in a huge pot over medium heat. Add the onion, ½ teaspoon salt, and a few toils of pepper, and cook, blending sporadically, for 8 minutes. Add the carrot and yam, mix and cook 2 additional minutes.
2. Add the wine and cook for around 30 seconds to lessen significantly, at that point add the canned tomatoes, garlic, oregano, and red pepper drops. Mix in the stock and narrows leaves. Heat to the point of boiling, at that point lessen the heat to a stew and cook, covered, for 20 minutes.
3. Mix in the cherry tomatoes, green beans, zucchini, chickpeas, and cover and cook 10 to 15 additional minutes, until the green beans are delicate.
4. Mix in the vinegar, kale, an extra ½ teaspoon salt (or to taste), and more pepper.
5. Vegetable Soup Recipe Variation Tips:
6. I require a ton of vegetables in this soup, yet utilize whatever you have close by as well as skip what you don't have. Here are a couple of simple approaches to switch things up:
7. Utilize all carrot or all yam rather than both, or add butternut squash all things being equal.
8. Throw in a couple cut cremini mushrooms when you add the carrot.
9. Trade ringer pepper for the cherry tomatoes, zucchini, or green beans.
10. Utilize another verdant green, similar to spinach or chard, instead of the kale.

11. Embellishment bowls with finely chopped parsley or basil, a scoop of pesto, or sprinkle of Parmesan cheddar!

35. Chickpea Salad Sandwich

Prep time20 mins Cook time5 mins Total time25 mins Serves: 3-4

Ingredients:

- Chickpea Salad
- 1½ cups cooked chickpeas, depleted and washed
- 2 tablespoons tahini
- 1 teaspoon Dijon mustard
- ½ garlic clove
- 1 teaspoon tricks
- 1 green onion, chopped
- 2 tablespoons chopped cilantro
- 2 tablespoons new lemon juice
- ocean salt and newly ground dark pepper
- For the sandwiches
- modest bunch of flimsy green beans, managed
- 1 delicate roll, cut fifty-fifty
- 8 to 10 Kalamata olives, hollowed and cut into equal parts
- meagerly cut red onion, washed and dried
- vegetarian mayo (or normal mayo), for spreading

- ¼ English cucumber, meagerly cut
- 1 radish, meagerly cut
- 6 to 8 new basil leaves
- ocean salt and newly ground dark pepper

Guidelines

1. Make the chickpea salad: In a food processor, consolidate the chickpeas, tahini, Dijon mustard, garlic, escapades, green onions, cilantro, lemon squeeze, and portions of salt and pepper. Heartbeat until consolidated, yet don't puree. Season to taste.
2. Whiten the green beans. Heat a little pot of salted water to the point of boiling and spot a bowl of ice water close by. Drop the green beans into the bubbling water for 1½ minutes, at that point scoop into the ice water to stop the cooking cycle. When cool, channel, wipe off, and slash into 1-inch pieces.
3. Amass the sandwiches: Spread the chickpea salad on one side of the loaf. Press the chopped green beans into the chickpea salad and top with the olives and red onion cuts. Spread of layer of mayo on the other portion of the roll and top with the cut cucumbers, radishes, and basil. Season with salt and pepper, to taste. Press together, cut, and enjoy!
4. Chickpea Salad Sandwich Serving Suggestions
5. This chickpea salad sandwich is a fabulous work day lunch! On the off chance that you need to prepare it ahead of time, make the chickpea blend early and store it in an impermeable compartment in the refrigerator

for as long as 3 days. Amass the sandwich on the morning of the day (or days) you intend to eat it. Head to this post to track down my best tips for preparing and pressing sandwiches to take in a hurry!

6. This formula is additionally superb outing admission. Enjoy it all alone, or pair it with a new serving of mixed greens like my pasta salad, broccoli salad, cucumber salad, or Greek serving of mixed greens. For additional serving thoughts, look at this post for my main 37 plate of mixed greens recipes. Enjoy!

36. Easy Power Lunch Bowls

serves 2 Prep time: 20 min Cook time: 10 min

Ingredients:

- 1 little yam, cubed
- 8 Yves Kale and Quinoa Bites
- ¾ cup cooked chickpeas, depleted and washed
- 1 tablespoon extra-virgin olive oil, in addition to additional for showering
- 1 lemon
- ¼ teaspoon Dijon mustard
- 8 to 10 lacinato kale leaves, chopped
- 6 paper-slight cuts from 1 Chioggia beet or watermelon radish
- ½ avocado, diced (optional)
- 1 tablespoon hemp seeds
- Red pepper pieces (optional)
- 2 tablespoons runny tahini (slight with warm water if necessary)**
- Ocean salt and newly ground dark pepper

Guidelines:

1. Preheat the oven to 400°F and fix a heating sheet with material paper. Throw the yams with a shower of olive oil and portions of salt and pepper and meal for 25 minutes. Partially through add the Yves Kale and Quinoa Bites to the heating sheet.
2. In the interim, in a little bowl, join the chickpeas, 1 tablespoon olive oil, 1 tablespoon lemon juice, Dijon mustard and portions of salt and pepper. Put away.
3. In an enormous bowl, knead the kale with a shower of olive oil, ½ tablespoon lemon juice and a spot of salt and pepper. We're preparing each layer here to ensure the entirety of the vegetables are delightful.
4. Gather two enormous individual serving bowls with the kale, chickpeas, yams, Yves Kale and Quinoa Bites, beet or radish cuts and avocado, if using. Sprinkle with the hemp seeds and red pepper pieces, if using. Sprinkle with the tahini sauce and another enormous crush of lemon, whenever wanted. Present with lemon wedges.
5. **Notes:**
6. **If you don't adore the flavor of crude tahini, or if yours preferences severe without anyone else, make a dressing by combining the accompanying ingredients as one:
7. 2 tablespoons tahini
8. ½ tablespoon apple juice vinegar or lemon juice
9. ½ teaspoon maple syrup
10. 1 to 2 tablespoons warm water, depending on the situation
11. Ocean salt and newly ground dark pepper

37. Beet Hummus

***Prep time*10 mins *Cook time*40 mins *Total time*50 mins**

Primary Ingredients:

- Beets. Broil them at 400 until fork delicate.
- Garlic. It adds kick and profundity of flavor.
- Chickpeas. It wouldn't be hummus without them!
- Tahini and extra-virgin olive oil. Add them to get a smooth, rich last plunge.
- Warm water. Simply a sprinkle extricates the plunge, so it mixes to rich flawlessness.
- Cumin and coriander. I show them as optional, yet I strongly prescribe using the flavors to give the hummus scrumptious profundity of flavor.
- Ocean salt and new dark pepper. The last final details!
- Serves: 1½ cups
- Ingredients
- 1 medium or 2 little red beets
- 2 garlic cloves

- 1½ cups cooked chickpeas, depleted and flushed
- 2 tablespoons tahini
- 2 tablespoons extra-virgin olive oil
- 2 tablespoons new lemon juice
- 2 to 3 tablespoons warm water
- ½ teaspoon every one of cumin and coriander (optional)
- Ocean salt and newly ground dark pepper
- Present with:
- 1 little roll, cut and toasted
- Radishes, cut down the middle (or other crude veggies)
- 1 teaspoon sesame seeds
- 1 tablespoon chopped parsley
- 1 tablespoon pine nuts

Directions:
1. Preheat the oven to 400°F. Shower the beet with olive oil and afterward wrap the beet and garlic together in foil. Spot on the heating sheet and dish 30 to 40 minutes, or until the beet is fork-delicate.
2. At the point when adequately cool to deal with, strip the beet skins under running water using your hands. Slash the beet and spot it in a blender. Add the cooked garlic, chickpeas, tahini, olive oil, lemon squeeze, and water and mix until smooth. Add cumin and coriander, in the event that you like. Chill until prepared to utilize.
3. Slather onto loaf and trimming with sesame seeds, pine nuts and parsley (all optional), or present with firm crude veggies.

Notes:
Make this sans gluten by using sans gluten wafers rather than roll.

38. Veggie Noodles

Prep Time: 10 mins Total Time: 5 mins Serves 2

Ingredients:
- Pick a vegetable:
- Butternut squash
- Beet
- Cucumber
- Carrot
- Daikon radish
- Summer squash
- Kohlrabi
- Yam
- Zucchini

Directions:
1. Butternut squash noodles: Look for a squash with a long neck. Hack off the fat, decrepit base of the squash and save it for another utilization (see ideas in the post above). Strip the squash and utilize a spiralizer to make noodles.
2. Beet noodles: Look for a large beet. Strip off the skin and utilize a spiralizer to make noodles.

3. Cucumber noodles: Look for a large English cucumber. Utilize a spiralizer or julienne peeler to make noodles (no compelling reason to strip).
4. Carrot noodles: Look for a fat carrot. Clean well or strip if it's excessively grimy. Utilize a spiralizer or julienne peeler to make noodles.
5. Daikon noodles: Use a spiralizer to make noodles.
6. Summer squash noodles: Look for a large yellow squash. Utilize a spiralizer or julienne peeler to make noodles. Or on the other hand utilize a normal vegetable peeler and strip into thick lace formed noodles. There's no compelling reason to strip the skin of the squash.
7. Kohlrabi noodles: Chop the greens off and put something aside for another utilization. Strip off any nubby parts from the kohlrabi bulb. Utilize a spiralizer to make noodles.
8. Yam noodles: Look for a thick yam. Strip the yam and utilize a spiralizer to make noodles.
9. Zucchini noodles: Look for a large zucchini. Utilize a spiralizer or julienne peeler to make noodles. Or on the other hand utilize a customary vegetable peeler and strip into thick lace formed noodles. There's no compelling reason to strip the skin of the zucchini.
10. Noddles serving ideas and tips
11. Butternut Squash Noodles
12. To make butternut squash noodles, search for a squash with a long neck. Slash off the fat, undesirable base of the squash, yet don't throw it! It's not ideal for making veggie noodles, but

rather you can in any case cook it or transform it into soup.

13. Butternut squash noodles are one of only a handful few sorts of vegetable noodles that I cook. Delicately sauté them with a sprinkle of olive oil until they mollify marginally. This lone requires a little while – the noodles should keep a pleasant still somewhat firm chomp. At that point, it's an ideal opportunity to eat. Here are a couple of my #1 approaches to serve them:

14. In a plant-put together riff with respect to spaghetti and meatballs. Top the noodles with marinara sauce, vegetarian meatballs, and veggie lover Parmesan cheddar.

15. Instead of the customary noodles in my Easy Pesto Pasta. Serve them with exemplary basil pesto or vegetarian pesto and delicate greens like spinach or arugula.

16. In an all-veggie riff on Spaghetti Aglio e Olio. Throw the noodles with sautéed garlic and kale, red pepper drops, lemon zing, lemon juice, and vegetarian Parmesan or customary Parmesan cheddar.

17. Cucumber Noodles

18. These cool cucumber noodles are so invigorating on blistering mid year days! I like to make them out of English cucumbers, as they're less watery than other cucumber assortments. Throw them with tahini sauce or nut sauce, new mint or cilantro, and heated tofu or tempeh for a quick bite,

19. Daikon Radish Veggie Noodles

20. Daikon veggie noodles have a delightful peppery chomp and still somewhat firm surface.

In light of its pale, clear appearance, I like to utilize white daikon radish as a substitute for rice noodles, however purple daikon or watermelon radish works superbly as well. Throw crude radish noodles with tahini sauce or nut sauce and prepared tofu or tempeh

21. Spiralized Kohlrabi
22. Not certain how to manage the kohlrabi in your CSA box? Spiralize it! Use kohlrabi noodles rather than the kohlrabi matchsticks in this noodle salad, or trade them in for the daikon noodles in my Spiralized Daikon "Rice Noodle" Bowl. In case you're searching for additional approaches to serve them, attempt any of these ideas:
23. Shower them with tahini sauce. Sprinkle cooked chickpeas, diced tomatoes, diced cucumbers, parsley, and mint on top.
24. Daintily sauté them and throw them with marinara sauce or rich pomodoro sauce. Add a couple of vegetarian meatballs to balance the dinner.
25. Throw them with nut sauce, prepared tofu or tempeh, and squashed peanuts or cashews. A modest bunch of new mint and a shower of gochujang sauce will take these veggie noodles over the top.

39. Sautéed Beet Greens

Prep Time: 3 minsCook Time: 2 minsTotal Time: 5 mins Serves 2 to 4

Ingredients:

- 1 pack beet greens
- 1 teaspoon extra-virgin olive oil
- 1 garlic clove, finely chopped
- 2 tablespoons brilliant raisins
- Lemon wedge
- 1 tablespoon chopped pecans or pistachios
- Ocean salt and newly ground dark pepper

Directions:

1. Separate the stems from the beet greens. Finely slash the stems and coarsely hack the leaves.
2. Heat the oil in a large skillet over medium heat. Add the garlic and the beet stems and cook, blending, for 1 moment. Add the beet greens, a couple of portions of salt and newly ground dark pepper, and sauté, throwing, until just shriveled.

3. Mood killer the heat, add the raisins, a major press of lemon, and throw. Move to a platter, top with the pecans and season to taste with more salt and pepper.
4. Best Beet Greens Recipe Tips
5. Clasp them immediately. To expand the existence of both the beets and greens, cut the greens from their underlying foundations when you return home from the ranchers market or store. Something else, the greens will pull dampness from the beets, causing them to shrink rapidly. After you cut the greens, envelop them by plastic or a reusable produce sack and store them in the crisper cabinet of your ice chest until you're prepared to cook them.
6. Wash them well. At the store, you'll once in a while discover beet greens that are pre-washed and prepared to-eat. As far as I can tell, they're normally the inverse: canvassed in earth! Continuously, consistently wash and dry beet greens before you cook them to eliminate any soil or flotsam and jetsam.
7. Utilize the stems just as the leaves. Like Swiss chard, beet leaves have fresh, consumable stems that add tone and mash to any beet greens formula. Try not to throw them! Finely dice them and cook them directly alongside the leaves.

40. Beet Recipes: Simple Alkaline Roasted Beets

Prep Time: 15 mins Cook Time: 45 mins Total Time: 1hr Serves 4

Ingredients:

- 6 to 8 little or medium red or yellow beets
- Extra-virgin olive oil, for showering
- 1 large navel orange
- Sherry vinegar or balsamic vinegar, for showering
- Juice of ½ lemon, or to taste
- Modest bunch of watercress leaves, or arugula or microgreens
- Ocean salt and newly ground dark pepper
- Flaky ocean salt, optional

Directions:

1. Preheat the oven to 400°F.
2. Spot every beet on a piece of foil and sprinkle liberally with olive oil and portions of ocean salt and newly ground dark pepper. Enclose the beets by the foil and meal on a heating

sheet for 35 to an hour, or until delicate and fork-delicate. The time will rely upon the size and newness of the beets. Eliminate the beets from the oven, eliminate the foil, and put away to cool. At the point when they are cool to the touch, strip the skins. I like to hold them under running water and slide the skins off with my mind.

3. Utilize a citrus peeler to strip long strips around the orange, keeping away from the white essence. Ground zing would work here too. Cut ¾ of the orange into fragments and save the excess ¼ wedge for crushing.

4. Cut the beets into 1" wedges or lumps and spot them in a bowl. In case you're using red and yellow beets, place each tone into discrete dishes so the red beets don't stain the yellow beets.

5. Sprinkle with olive oil and sherry vinegar, at that point add the lemon juice, squeezed orange crushed from the leftover wedge, and a couple of portions of salt and pepper and throw. Chill until prepared to serve.

6. Taste prior to serving and season with more salt (flaky ocean salt, if using) and pepper or more vinegar (for more tang), orange, or lemon juice, as wanted.

7. Serve on a platter with the orange fragments, watercress, and citrus twists.

41. Shakshuka with Swiss Chard

Total: 1hr Yield: 4

Ingredients:

- Fixing Checklist
- 3 tablespoons extra-virgin olive oil
- 4 ounces substantial bacon, minced
- 1 medium onion, minced
- 4 garlic cloves, minced
- 1 large bundle Swiss chard, stems minced and leaves saved
- 32 ounces (4 cups) arranged pureed tomatoes
- 1 teaspoon dried basil
- Spot of squashed red pepper
- Fit salt
- Newly ground dark pepper
- 8 large eggs
- 3 tablespoons newly ground Parmigiano-Reggiano cheddar
- 1/4 cup meagerly cut basil leaves

Directions:
1. Preheat the oven to 350°. In a large ovenproof skillet, heat the olive oil. Add the bacon, onion, garlic and chard stems and cook over moderate heat, blending incidentally, until the stems are softened, around 5 minutes. Add the pureed tomatoes, dried basil and squashed red pepper and stew until the sauce is thickened, around 15 minutes. Season with salt and pepper.
2. In the mean time, in a large pot of salted bubbling water, whiten the chard leaves for 3 minutes. Channel and let cool marginally. Crush out the overabundance water. Structure the chard leaves into 8 little heaps and orchestrate them in the sauce around the side the skillet.
3. Break the eggs into the skillet between the heaps of chard. Move the skillet to the oven and heat the eggs for 12 to 15 minutes, until the egg whites are simply set and the yolks are as yet runny.
4. Move the skillet to a rack and sprinkle the cheddar on top. Let represent 5 minutes. Enhancement the shakshuka with the cut basil and serve right away.

42. Swiss Chard Tart

Prep time: 25 MINUTES cook time: 30 MINUTES total time: 55 MINUTES

INGREDIENTS:

FOR THE TART DOUGH:

- ¼ cup/30 g pine nuts
- ¼ cup/30g custard flour
- 1 3/4 cups/196g almond flour
- 1/2 tsp ocean salt
- 2 Tablespoons/30g coconut oil or ghee or margarine
- 1 egg white (save the yolk for the filling)
- FOR THE TART FILLING:
- 1 Tablespoon/15ml additional virgin olive oil
- 2 little garlic cloves, finely chopped
- ¼ teaspoon red pepper drops
- 1 large bundle of swiss chard, generally chopped (leaves just) with water actually sticking to the leaves
- 3 eggs in addition to 1 egg yolk
- 1/2 cup/120ml entire milk yogurt (ideally sheep's milk) or (plain coconut yogurt for paleo)
- ½ teaspoon ocean salt

- ¼ teaspoon newly ground dark pepper
- 1 Tablespoon currants or raisins (optional)
- 2 Tablespoons/60g pine nuts, toasted
- 1 to 2 oz sheep's milk feta cheddar (overlook for paleo)

Directions:
1. MAKE THE TART DOUGH:
2. Preheat oven to 350 degrees F.
3. Interaction the pine nuts and custard flour in a food processor until you have a fine flour. Add the almond flour , salt and ghee or coconut oil and heartbeat to consolidate. With the engine running add the egg white through the shoot and interaction until a brittle batter begins to frame.
4. Assemble the batter with your hands and spot it in the focal point of a delicately lubed 9-inch tart container squeezing it out equally to the edges and up the edge of the tart dish using your fingers and the palm of your hand. Prick the batter done with the tins of a fork and refrigerate to firm for at any rate 20 to 30 minutes or spot in the cooler for 10 minutes prior to heating.
5. Heat for 15 to 18 minutes until delicately brilliant and set.
6. Eliminate from oven and cool on wire rack while making the filling.
7. MAKE THE TART FILLING:
8. Heat the oven to 350 degrees F.
9. Heat the olive oil, garlic and red pepper pieces over medium heat in a medium measured skillet

or sauté prospect minute until fragrant however not brown.

10. Add the chard and coat with the oil and flavors. Cover halfway and cook until delicate (around 5 to 7 minutes), blending as fundamental and adding a Tablespoon of water if the leaves look excessively dry. Put away to cool while you make the custard.

11. Beat the eggs in a large bowl with the yogurt and salt and pepper. Mix in the chard combination and currants.

12. Empty the filling into the tart and dissipate the pine nuts (and feta if using) over the surface. Prepare until brilliant and firm, (around 30 to 35 minutes) covering the edge of the outside with foil as fundamental if browning excessively fast.

13. Allow cool totally on a wire to rack and serve at room temperature.

43. Rainbow Chard Soup

Prep time: 10 min Servings 2 servings

Ingredients:

- 2 tablespoons spread
- 1 fennel bulb
- 10 scallions, roots managed, white and light green parts chopped, some dull green parts held
- 2 garlic cloves, finely chopped
- 1/2 jalapeño, stem eliminated, finely chopped (I incorporated the seeds and ribs for heat)
- 7 ounces full-fat coconut milk (around 1/2 a can)
- 2 1/4 cups water
- 1 pack (3/4 pound) rainbow chard, stems eliminated and saved, leaves chopped
- 1 teaspoon genuine salt, in addition to additional to taste
- 1 small bunch of child spinach leaves
- Lemon juice

- Optional fixings: Greek yogurt (or creme fraiche or acrid cream), toasted chopped almonds, toasted coconut pieces, cut scallion greens, cured chard stems (see formula beneath)

Directions:
1. Trim the stalks and the root end of the fennel. Hold a portion of the fennel fronds, yet dispose of stalks and intense root. Slice the fennel bulb down the middle, and cut out the center. Dispose of center. Cleave remaining fennel into 1/2-inch pieces.
2. Warm margarine in a medium pan over medium heat. Add chopped fennel, scallion, garlic and jalapeño, and saute until the fennel begins to mollify (around 5 minutes). Add coconut milk, and stew for 2 minutes. Add water, rainbow chard leaves and salt, and cook until the leaves are delicate (around 5 minutes).
3. Move soup to a blender with a small bunch of infant spinach leaves, and mix until smooth. You can add a little water if the soup is excessively thick. Season to taste with lemon juice (around 1/2 a lemon) and extra salt.
4. To serve, split soup between 2 dishes (course) or 4 dishes (starter), and top with Greek yogurt, toasted chopped almonds, toasted coconut pieces, cut scallion greens, and salted chard stems.

44. Potato pancakes with chard

Prep: 10 mins Cook: 15 mins Easy Serves 2

Ingredients:

- 300g crushed potato
- 4 spring onions , finely chopped
- 25g plain wholemeal flour
- ½ tsp preparing powder
- 3 eggs
- 2 tsp rapeseed oil
- 240g chard , stalks and leaves generally chopped, or infant spinach, chopped

Strategy:

1. Blend the crush, spring onions, flour, preparing powder and 1 of the eggs in a bowl. Heat the oil in a non-stick skillet, at that point spoon in the potato blend to make two hills. Level them to frame two 15cm plates and fry for 5-8 mins until the undersides are set and brilliant, at that point cautiously ip over and cook on the opposite side.

2. In the interim, wash the chard and put in a dish with a portion of the water actually sticking to it, at that point cover and cook over

a medium heat for 5 mins until shriveled and delicate. Poach the excess eggs.

3. Top the flapjacks with the greens and egg. Serve while the yolks are as yet runny. Works out positively For Eggy bread Banana, coconut and cardamom bread Chorizo and halloumi breakfast loaf

45. Swiss chard & kohlrabi with lemon sauce

Total time30 mins Ready in 30 mins more effort serves 4 – 6

Ingredients:
- 1bunch Swiss chard (about 500g)
- 1 lemon , ground zing and pressed juice
- 1 kohlrabi , stripped and split
- 300ml vegetable stock
- 2 tbsp chopped new parsley
- 100ml olive oil
- large twigs new rosemary , tarragon, coriander and parsley
- 2-3 garlic cloves

Strategy:
1. Cut the white chard comes from green leaves in a V shape, cut slantingly into 5mm strips. Cut the leaves fifty-fifty, move 3-4 all at once like a

stogie, daintily cut. Put in a bowl and dissipate with a little lemon zing. Meagerly cut kohlrabi and sprinkle with zing too.

2. Heat up the stock and lemon juice to decrease significantly. Pour in a container and blend in the chopped parsley. Cool, race in the vast majority of the oil.

3. Put the rosemary, tarragon and coriander into a steaming dish with the garlic. Cover with water and bring to the bubble. Fit container on top. Sprinkle base with salt and pepper and lay in the kohlrabi. Dissipate over white chard and season once more. Top with the twigs of parsley. Sprinkle with oil, cover and steam, 5 mins. Eliminate parsley and dissipate over the green chard, lifting up the white vegetables softly with a large fork. Cover and steam for 3-4 additional mins.

4. Eliminate to a serving dish and pour over some sauce to serve. This preferences superb with barbecued salmon or a chicken bosom.

5. Formula TIPS:

6. GORDON'S SECRETS OF SUCCESS

7. Incredible for securing vegetables and keeping all the decency in

8. GORDON'S SECRETS OF SUCCESS

9. Pick sensitive vegetables for steaming

10. GORDON'S SECRETS OF SUCCESS

11. Put any extra spices in the water for steaming as it will assist with perfuming your vegetables

46. Baked Swiss chard

Prep: 15 mins Cook:40 mins Easy Serves 6

Ingredients:
- Oil or spread, for lubing
- 1kg Swiss chard , stems cut into 1cm pieces and leaves into quarters
- 200ml twofold cream
- 1 garlic clove , squashed to a paste with ocean salt
- 2 egg yolks
- 200g parmesan , ground (or veggie lover elective)
- 75g dried breadcrumbs
- 1 tsp new thyme leaves

Strategy:
1. Put a container of salted water on to bubble and cook the chard stalks for 2 mins until delicate. Eliminate the stalks with an opened spoon. Add the leaves and cook for 30 secs-1 min. Channel and save 200ml of the cooking water. In a pan, carry the cream to a stew, at that point add the garlic and cook for 2 mins. Race in the water, egg yolks and 140g Parmesan, and let them all soften together and bubble for 3 mins.

2. Heat oven to 180C/160C fan/gas 4. Add the chard to the pot, season, blend well and tip into a lubed heating dish. Top with the breadcrumbs, thyme and remaining Parmesan. Cover with thwart and heat for 15 mins. Remove the foil and cook for 15 mins more until brilliant and percolating.
3. Works out in a good way For Semolina broil potatoes with garlic and thyme
4. Sheep shoulder with cove leaves and juniper berries
5. Chocolate torta della nonna

47. Swiss chard gratin

Prep: 15 mins Cook: 40 mins plus cooling more effort Serves 4

Ingredients:
- 400g Swiss chard
- 3 star anise
- 200g brilliant caster sugar
- 300g white wine vinegar
- 1 tbsp coriander seeds
- 1 tbsp white pepper
- 1 tbsp fennel seeds
- 300ml pot twofold cream
- 3 garlic cloves , ground
- 100g gruyère , ground
- great touch of cayenne pepper

Strategy:

1. To pickle the chard, put 400ml water in a large pot or sauté container with the star anise, sugar and vinegar. Put the leftover flavors in a material pack attached with string, add to the dish, bring to the bubble, at that point drop in the chard, tail first. Press the chard down in the skillet and stew for 3-4 mins – don't stress on the off chance that you can't cover the leaves totally in the fluid, as they will shrink and get lowered while cooking. Eliminate the skillet from the heat and leave to cool.

2. Heat oven to 180C/160C fan/gas 4. Once cooled, eliminate the chard from the pickle blend and wipe off with a spotless kitchen towel. Lay the chard in an A4-sized preparing dish. In a bowl, whisk the cream and garlic along with some flavoring, at that point pour over the chard. Sprinkle over the cheddar and cayenne pepper, and prepare for 30 mins.

3. Works out in a good way For Brown margarine poached halibut with celeriac purée and escapade scraps

4. Rack of venison, cooked carrots and forager sauce

5. Poached halibut with legacy tomatoes

48. Fudgy fig roll

Prep: 1hr Cook: 12 mins - 15 mins plus softening and cooling More effort Cuts into 10 slices

Ingredients:

- 140g soft dried fig , chopped
- 1 medium very ripe banana
- knob of butter , for greasing
- 3 large eggs , separated
- 225g light muscovado sugar
- 120g wholemeal flour
- 1 tsp bicarbonate of soda
- 1 tsp ground cinnamon
- good grating fresh nutmeg (optional)
- 4 tbsp golden caster sugar
- For the filling
- 300ml double cream
- 4 tbsp icing sugar , sifted
- about 250-300g fig jam or conserve

Method:

1. Cover the figs with boiling water in a bowl and set aside to soften for 30 mins. Drain and mash well with the banana.

2. Heat oven to 190C/170C fan/gas 5. Grease a Swiss roll tin – about 34 x 24cm. Line the base with baking parchment.
3. Separate the eggs, collecting the whites in a large clean bowl. Beat with an electric whisk until stiff peaks hold on the end of your whisk, then add half the sugar and beat until thick and glossy.
4. In another mixing bowl, beat the yolks with the remaining sugar until pale. Whisk in the mashed fig mixture. Fold this mixture into the meringue mixture until well combined. Mix the flour, bicarbonate of soda, spices and a pinch of salt. Sprinkle it over the wet mixture and very gently fold in, again until well combined. Gently scrape and spread the batter into the tin. Bake for 12-15 mins until springy to the touch.
5. Meanwhile, lay a clean tea towel on the bench (this helps keep the cake nice and moist). Scatter the caster sugar over the towel, flip on the cake, peel off the parchment, then roll up from the shortest side with the tea towel into a Swiss roll. Lift onto a wire rack to cool completely.
6. Unroll the cake gently. Using electric beaters, whisk the cream and icing sugar together to soft peaks. Spread the fig jam over the cake, followed by the cream. Roll up again and slice to serve.
7. **RECIPE TIPS**
8. BANANAS NOT RIPE ENOUGH?
9. Stick one in the freezer – overnight is ideal – then gently defrost in the microwave (or at

room temp) the next day. It should now be squishy, perfect for making a cake.

49. Chard, sweet potato & peanut stew

Prep: 15 mins Cook: 45 mins Easy Serves 4
Ingredients
- 2 tbsp sunflower oil
- 1 large onion , chopped
- 1 tsp cumin seeds
- 400g yams , cut into medium lumps
- ½ tsp squashed bean stew chips
- 400g can chopped tomato
- 140g salted, cooked peanuts
- 250g chard , leaves and stems, washed and generally chopped

Technique:
1. Heat a large pan with a top over a medium heat and add the oil. Add the onion and fry until light brilliant. Mix in the cumin seeds until fragrant, around 1 min, at that point add the yam, bean stew chips, tomatoes and 750ml water. Mix, cover and bring to the bubble, at that point uncover and stew for 15 mins.
2. In the mean time, whizz the peanuts in a food processor until finely ground, yet stop before

you end up with peanut butter. Add them to the stew, mix and taste for preparing – you might need to add a squeeze more salt. Stew for a further 15 mins, blending as often as possible.

3. At last, mix in the chard. Get back to the bubble and stew, covered, mixing at times, for 8-10 mins or until the chard is cooked. Serve steaming hot with a lot of newly ground dark pepper.

4. Works out in a good way For

5. Sugar plums

50. ribbons tossed with chard

Prep: 20 mins Cook: 15 mins More effort Serves 2

Ingredients:

- 1 little celeriac , stripped
- 1 lemon , squeezed
- 40g pumpkin seeds
- 2 tbsp additional virgin olive oil
- 15g spread
- 4 thyme twigs , leaves eliminated
- 2 finely chopped cloves of garlic
- ½ tsp of dried stew pieces
- 1 pack of chard , leaves isolated from stalks, stalks cut and leaves shredded
- 20g pecorino

Strategy:

1. Using a decent vegetable peeler, cut long, wide strips (about the width of pappardelle) around the periphery of the celeriac, into a bowl of

water and lemon juice, until you have heaps of strips. Consider more than you would if using pasta.

2. Dry-fry the pumpkin seeds in a container until they've puffed and popped. Put away.
3. Bring a large container of salted water to the bubble. Add the celeriac for 1 min, channel and save the water. In a non-stick griddle, heat the oil and spread until the margarine has dissolved and frothed up. Add the thyme, garlic and bean stew.
4. Cook the garlic blend for 5 mins until fragrant and practically brilliant, add the chard stalks and mix, cooking for a couple more mins. Add the pumpkin seeds and the chard leaves, season and crush in some lemon juice. Turn up the heat and mix into equal parts the ground cheddar. Add the celeriac and a slosh of the cooking water and throw, shaking the dish until the sauce looks polished. Split between plates, top with more cheddar and serve.
5. **Formula TIPS:**
6. ARE PUMPKIN SEEDS HEALTHY?
7. Pumpkin seeds are plentiful in crucial nutrients and minerals.

51. Cherry & almond frangipane galette

Prep: 30 mins Cook: 45 mins plus chilling and cooling Easy Serves 4-6

Ingredients:

- 400g cherries , pitted and split
- 1 tsp caster sugar
- 1 tbsp lemon juice
- 3 tbsp morello cherry save
- 1 egg , beaten
- 2 tbsp granulated sugar
- thickened cream , to serve (optional)
- For the baked good
- 200g white spelt flour
- 1 tbsp caster sugar
- 120g unsalted margarine , chilled and cut into blocks
- For the frangipane
- 100g entire, skin-on almonds , toasted

- 15g unsalted spread
- 1 tbsp spelt flour , in addition to extra for tidying
- ½ tsp vanilla substance
- 50g brilliant caster sugar
- 1 egg

Technique:

1. To start with, make the cake. Filter the flour into a bowl and mix in the sugar and a touch of salt. Add the margarine and focus on it with your fingertips until you have a coarse scrap consistency. Mix in 2-3 tbsp of super cold water and unite the combination with your hands. Manipulate it against the side of the bowl, and on the off chance that it meets up easily, squash it into a ball. In the event that it's actually disintegrating, add somewhat more frosted water and work it until you have a flexible baked good batter. Envelop it by preparing material and chill for 30 mins. Then, macerate the cherries in the sugar and lemon juice in a bowl.
2. To make the frangipane, rush the almonds in a food processor until finely chopped, at that point add the spread, flour, vanilla concentrate and sugar, and barrage until joined. Add the egg, and barrage again to make a paste.
3. Heat oven to 160C/140C fan/gas 3. On a gently floured surface, carry out the cake into a large circle about 30cm wide, and the thickness of a pound coin. It doesn't make any difference if the edges are parted. Slide onto a heating sheet fixed with preparing material,

and spread over the preserve, leaving about a 4cm line right around the edge. Cover this with the frangipane, at that point press a large portion of the cherries into it. Overlay over the baked good edges to encase the edges of the cherries, pushing down the wrinkles so it holds together. Brush with the beaten egg and dissipate some granulated sugar over the cherries and baked good. Put in the cooler for 10 mins.

4. Prepare the galette for 45 mins, at that point eliminate from the oven and permit to cool for 10-15 mins. Pour over the leftover new cherries and spoon over any juices. Present with thickened cream, on the off chance that you like.

52. Vanilla poached pears with almond butter porridge topping

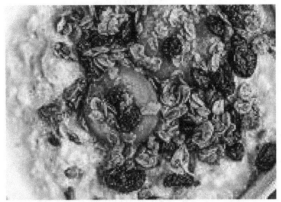

Prep: 10 mins Cook: 20 mins Easy Serves 2

Ingredients:
- 2 little pears
- 100g caster sugar
- juice of ½ a lemon
- 1 vanilla unit (then again, utilize 1 tsp vanilla bean paste)
- 1 tbsp almond spread
- toasted chipped almonds

Strategy:
1. Strip, split and center the pears. Blend the sugar and lemon squeeze in with 200ml water in a little pot. Divide the vanilla case and scratch the seeds into the dish, at that point add the unit (or add the vanilla bean paste). Heat until the sugar has broken up.

2. Add the pears and cover the surface with a circle of preparing material (this will guarantee the pears cook through equally). Cook for 15-20 mins until the pears feel delicate when jabbed with a blade, at that point leave to cool. Can be saved chilled in the fluid for as long as multi week.
3. In the mean time, make your porridge. Blend the almond spread with sufficient poached pear fluid to frame a sprinkling consistency, at that point spoon over the porridge and top the dishes with the pears. Dissipate with the toasted chipped almonds.

Conclusion

I would like to thank you for going through all the recipes. These incorporate certain health benefits and are perfect for people who love to be on alkaline diet .These will help you in weight reduction. Try at home and enjoy

CPSIA information can be obtained
at www.ICGtesting.com
Printed in the USA
LVHW080715140621
690150LV00005B/94